Leadership
and the e-Learning Organization

Susan Smith Nash

Texture Press – 2006

Leadership
and the e-Learning Organization

Susan Smith Nash

ISBN: 0-9712061-6-3

Library of Congress Control Number: 2006902533

Texture Press
Guilderland, NY 12084

e-mail: texturepress@beyondutopia.com

Table of Contents

Vision and Leadership in the E-Learning Organization

Podcasts and e-Learning

Learning and Teaching Strategies that Work

In Hurricanes and Helicopters: E-Learners In Extremus

The Business of Distance and Flexible Courses and Programs

Please Make Me Think!
Creating Engaging and Relevant Online Courses

Management Issues in the E-Learning Organization

Leadership and the Future of the E-Learning Organization

Things won are done; joy's soul lies in the doing.
        William Shakespeare, *Troilus and Cressida,*
        Act 1, Scene 2

With thanks and appreciation for all those whom I have had the privilege to meet and to work with over the years.

Vision and Leadership in the E-Learning Organization

Appropriate Leadership for Learning Organizations

As learning organizations seek to expand their distance programs which include online and mobile technology-enabled delivery systems as well as hybrid, or blended solutions, and they endeavor to find the best and most appropriate use of technology, there is an increasing awareness that the strategic planning methods of the past are often inadequate.

Leadership theories that focus on managing change often do not directly address the clash between long-term constituencies who have unchanging long-term goals, and a radically and rapidly changing world. In such situations, the goals and desired outcomes may be fairly constant, but the methods of achieving them are constantly problematized by situational, financial and technological barriers and change. Scores of new books have claimed to offer the one sure remedy for dealing with change, while the latest and greatest leadership guru proffers up catchy one-size-fits-all catch-phrases. Slogans are good, but they are often inadequate when the problem is complex and a solution requires careful study and analysis.

Again, it is no exaggeration to say that there are literally thousands of books and articles on leadership. In this area, leadership theories continue to cross-pollinate across fields (military leadership lessons for business; business for military; ancient philosophers for modern leaders, etc.), the demand seems to be in no way satisfied. Although one can argue that leadership is a very hands-on, applied art, and that the lessons of history seem to be doomed to be disregarded, there seems to be a universal groundswell about leadership. If we study it enough, perhaps this time we'll get it right, seems to be the unstated message.

For the learning organization, this approach can be helpful, but unless the leadership issues are placed in real-world contexts, and the leadership challenges unique to a distributed, distant environment are honestly depicted, studying and applying examples from other fields can have disastrous results. The pitfalls of uncritically applying popular leadership lessons and theories from other fields or times are briefly discussed below.

Transformational Leadership. This is a theory that, when properly applied, can help a leader and team members bring out the best in each person, with very positive results in terms of achieving the mission and all desired outcomes. However, many influential writers have glamorized transformation and transformational leadership to the point that it has become almost synonymous with emotional catharsis combined with structural metamorphosis that follows the words pronounced by a charismatic leader.

The transformational leader, if some of the more enthusiastic apologists are to believed, can take any individual or group -- no matter or distant or disenfranchised -- and turn them into true believers, who are galvanized by an incontrovertible truth -- The Vision. In extreme cases, the vision is not arrived at through mutual buy-in or a team effort. Instead, it is pronounced by the leader.

Transformation in order to align oneself or one's unit to the vision is expected, even required, and team members must demonstrate evidence of their transformation, which can result in a kind of conformity that discourages risk-taking and creative problem-solving.

In the world of online and distance learning, rapid change required rapid response and the freedom to make decisions and changes at a very local level. Most adherents to the transformational leadership camp would claim that their approach allows individuals to enjoy freedom to think in non-conventional ways. However, closer examination reveals that a too-tight adherence to one interpretation of the vision will stifle creativity, and impose a political and/or ideological presence that was not there before.

Transactional Leadership. In today's world, it seems that no one wants to be a transactional leader. Transactional leadership is boring, because it focuses on workmanship-like process, and it defines itself in terms of actions. To those who have been completely seduced by the notion of self-actualization through transformational leadership, this is dull fare indeed. In this case, transactional leadership smacks of bureaucracy, with checklists of tasks and deadlines. However, in a distributed environment, sometimes transactional is the appropriate leadership style. By creating functional blocks of work, with clear tasks, and assigned responsibilities, it is possible to assign work to people in far-flung locations, separated by time zones and schedules.

Distributed Leadership. Leadership is distributed throughout the organization, and the role of leader changes constantly, depending upon the needs of the organization, or the task to be accomplished. In this case, the organization is broken down into functional units, or teams. Teams tend to be functional, and communities of practice tend to arise spontaneously, based in need, resources, and specific time constraints. Distributed leadership approaches are very effective in a setting where team members are moving constantly, and resources (information, financial, inputs) are also in flux.

In this case, to have positive results, it is important to very clearly define the desired outcomes so that each member fully understands what it is, how it can be measured, and how to go about developing a step-by-step procedure.

Leadership through Followership. According to this line of thinking about leadership, the followers in an organization both select and create their leader. They provide the mandate, as well as the muscle to get the job done. Further, because each leader was a follower once, he or she had to spend time in an apprenticeship phase. Understanding followership and the way that it gives individual team members a voice allows the members to share the common experience of followership, even while they are separated geographically, or are working in separate functional work units.

Leadership through Example. Military history is filled with leaders who died valiantly in battle, who overcame adverse conditions and personal injury to lead their troops to victory. The leader in a distributed education program will have very few opportunities (one would hope) to fall on an enemy grenade, or to use lethal force to cover critical troops or an objective. Nevertheless, there are similarities in the e-learning organization.

The leader can assume roles and take on tasks that demonstrate that he or she is willing to get into the trenches, and engage in the day to day operations of the enterprise. For example, the leader can demonstrate how he/she is willing to go to extreme lengths to make sure that the curriculum is developed, faculty are trained, students receive timely support, and that the infrastructure is in place and working is something team members can admire and emulate.

This chapter is a brief introduction to a broad topic, and one that will be explored in more depth in this book. Appropriate leadership is vital to the successful operation of a learning enterprise, and an eclectic yet tailored, situated approach is absolutely indispensable. Cross-pollination from other fields and the sayings and insights of historical thinkers are useful, too, but primarily when placed in context.

This book combines theory and practice, and it places great importance on showing examples. One goal of this book is to demonstrate how the leader becomes vital in the organization's discovery and implementation process.

Upward Mobility in the Distance Institution: Factors Influencing Prestige and Status in Online Programs

The college degree earned either partially or fully online has ascended in stature to solid respectability as college administrators have come to believe that online courses can be more rigorous than face-to-face. The popularity of online courses is accompanied by a newly emerging sense of prestige, which is on the verge of transforming the landscape of higher education by placing great cultural value on the method of delivery as well as the content.

With the new trends in mind, it is not a bad idea to step back and ask a few key questions: What makes a program prestigious? Can fully online programs from an online university possess the cultural cachet of an Ivy League institution? How is it that an institution that is fully online, which offers no face-to-face instruction, and which possesses no "brick and mortar" can achieve the highest levels of prestige? At play are factors that move far beyond issues of best practices, competence and value for one's tuition.

In order to achieve prestige as an online institution of higher education, one must understand the inner workings of status production in a society, and what constitutes cultural value. Social class determinations must be kept in mind, as well as the reasons for social stratification, and beliefs about upward mobility. Having a clear understanding of the relationship between education and social class has helped distance programs groom themselves to achieve higher levels of status. At the most basic level, however, the online program must contain a solid foundation of programs, as well as a coherent vision.

*A Vision That Begins and Ends with "Legacy"
Most institutions of higher learning have a vision statement that focuses principally on the here and now: what kind of classes, services, and experiences will the students have, and how will

they prepare them for a useful working life within a well-respected and stable community?

In contrast, the institution of higher learning that has achieved high status and prestige in society will tend to spend more time envisioning the distant future, clearly implying that individuals who have earned degrees from their institution are imbued with sufficient power and influence to bring about tangible change in the world. Without the proper context, the assumptions and articulated views will seem unrealistic, even narcissistic. However, when one realizes that a number of the graduating class will be influential policymakers and stakeholders within a specific social group, the underlying attitudes and assumptions seem less grandiose.

For the traditional high-prestige university, the academic year begins with a moment dedicated to envisioning the future: who will receive honorary doctorates? and who will be the perfect commencement speaker? At these moments, the participants communicate to each other, almost as though by osmosis, that this is an institution that not only prepares its students for a successful future, but also for powerful friends and influential connections.

What does the culminating moment look like for an online institution that has gained prestige and cultural status? The graduation ceremony should be seen for what it is: a rite of passage, a "launching" of graduates into the world. The influential speaker is the embodiment of achievement, influence, and deeply cherished values. For Thunderbird Garvin School of International Management, the MBA in International Management (http://www.thunderbird.edu/students/degree_prog/mbaim/)is a degree program that prides itself in continuing relations. Even as the graduates are launched, they are encouraged to keep in touch and to open doors for each other. It is worth noting that even before the advent of the Internet and Thunderbird's online program, Thunderbird graduates were well-received throughout the world. Their online program reinforces the notion that their perspective is truly global. The legacy is assumed to be a Thunderbird philosophy, an imprint on international business practices and policies, and a story of successful graduates.

For an online institution, the challenge is to communicate the same values and beliefs, but to do it in a visual manner. Careful attention must be paid to the visual details, with an eye to the semiotics – the coded non-verbal visual messages that convey complex messages.

*Tradition

While online programs have not existed for enough time to say that they are a part of a long tradition in and of themselves, it can be said that they are part of a continuum, and that the only difference is that of delivery method. For example, the University of Oklahoma has not offered an online graduate degree in museum studies for more than three or four years. On the other hand, two of the Southwest's largest and most prestigious museums -- the Sam Noble Natural History Museum and the Fred Jones Memorial Art Museum – have been mainstays of the university for decades. Thus, one can legitimately say that the online museum studies program is a part of a tradition. The fact that OU's Museum Studies courses are taught by University of Oklahoma curators and faculty also supports that supposition.

*Curriculum PLUS

In the new online universities, the curriculum is not only equivalent to traditional face-to-face programs, the online curriculum tends to exceed the face-to-face curriculum in terms of rigorous and regular review, and adherence to best practices. Online institutions take advantage of the distributed nature of course development and subject matter expertise, and bring together a collaboratively-created curriculum which incorporates elements from many sources, from many places. There is clear alignment with learner needs and desired outcomes.

The Sloan Consortium's report, *Growing By Degrees,* published in 2005, contains data that supports the growing perception that online education can be more rigorous and can contain more quality controls than face-to-face instruction. Despite the fact that most administrators believe that the quality of online instruction is more difficult to evaluate than face-to-face (2005), institutions continue to incorporate online instruction in their strategic plans. In 2005, fully 56% of responding institutions reported that online education was a critical component of their online strategy (2005).

In the case of Cornell University, a decision was made to focus on professional and executive development certificate programs through a new arm, eCornell. The University leveraged its reputation to bolster the credibility of the online programs. After successful launches of the program, several large, nationally known entities such as YMCA of the USA and Shangri-La Hotels and Resorts selected eCornell for employee development. (http://www.ecornell.com) Further, the programs have received national awards and commendations. Now it could even be said that the traditional part of Cornell University is benefiting from the reputation of eCornell.

*Instructional Materials in Multiple Formats
Instructional materials reflect the underlying values and defining vision of the institution. Instead of being dependent on the skill and passion of the face-to-face professor, the online institution dedicates resources to a team of developers who integrate content, vision, and values. The developers then adapt the material so that it can be delivered in a number of ways, which include text, audio, multimedia, and blended approaches.

To most effectively distribute the materials, the online program instructional designers must seek innovative ways to take advantage of the flexibility of the Internet, and develop materials that are deliverable at any time and at any place, using methods respected and recognized by others for their innovation. For example, online institutions can take advantage of mobile computing devices and have materials playable on portable mp3 players or video players, as well as have the distance materials be readable on small devices including laptops, palms, handhelds, and enhanced phones. However, delivery options should keep actual user needs in the forefront.

An example is Duke University, and its use of mobile computing and iPods to deliver content for students. While the iPods are used on campus and in hybrid settings where face-to-face instruction is blended with distance delivery, the audio files are also accessible for students in their online courses. The

iPods are used to listen to lectures and to record shareable content.
(http://www.chronicle.duke.edu/vnews/display.v/ART/2005/04/07/425512a814398)

*Collections of Rare Digital Resources
The university that enjoys prestige and high cultural status must have something unique that sets it apart from other colleges, universities, institutes, and think tanks. It should have at least one major collection of digital resources in which it exercises exclusive control and management. Obviously, there would be extensive sharing of the repository, and/or individuals would be able to subscribe. Examples could be an extensive collection of unique nature photos, scanned documents from a rare book collection, scanned images of historical manuscripts and journals, rare data collected from research, etc. The digital resources could also consist of software and cutting-edge programs.

Will sharing the resources detract from their status, and the belief that they are of high quality? Clearly, in some cases sharing, or making thing available via open-source software actually enhances the status. Cases include the Massachusetts Institute of Technology's OpenCourseWare project (http://ocw.mit.edu/index.html) and Stanford's LOCKSS (Lots of Copies Keeps Stuff Safe) program, which is a distributed digital archiving system
http://www.diglib.org/preserve/stanfordfinal.html. The common denominator is philanthropy, and the desire to be a leader in funding and implementing initiatives that provide access to educational technology and digital resources to at-risk populations. There are a few echoes of noblesse oblige, and this is, without a doubt, the digital equivalent of volunteerism and the "charity work" of the past. To state the obvious is not to be judgmental, simply to say that if it is not an update of a tried and true formula, the attempt probably will not work.

*Partnerships with solid, well-rounded organizations with depth and breadth
The online institution that aspires to achieve the level of "prestige" is cognizant of the fact that it cannot be done alone. Resource requirements are too steep. Further, to attempt to rise

by means of solitary efforts is ultimately futile because success requires partners, not only in terms of resources but also in areas of expertise and technical know-how. Partnering also allows the sharing of infrastructure and informational resources.

*Endowments and scholarship funds

The university that enjoys prestige, status, and high cultural value is notable for the way that it inspires individuals to contribute to the shared vision, and to support the making of a better world via a unique education. Prestigious universities are distinguished by their devotees – passionate alumni and true believers who are willing to endow scholarships, research, travel for students as well as for faculty.

In addition to private university grants and endowments used to support distance education endeavors, organizations such as the American Distance Education Consortium (ADEC) (http://www.adec.edu/) provides resources to support online program initiatives. Further, they publish lists of grantmakers, both federal and private, where competition is quite keen, and only high-quality proposals are awarded funding.

*Library

A robust digital library is an obvious requisite. It is important to possess not only subscriptions to databases, e-journals and indices, and other information products, but also digitized versions of rare books and statistical archives which can be used in research. Effective data-mining tools need to be in place as well, to help students and researchers effectively utilize the materials. Joining library and digital repository consortia when the materials truly enhance one's collection is an effective strategy. Working with government collections and having compatible systems is important, as is having well-trained staff who understand the nature of classification, intellectual property rights, etc. Learning object repositories are often useful components, but this area should be regarded with caution, since it is fairly easy to develop a repository of unusable, unmanageable, and unshareable digital objects without realizing it.

In addition to privately held digital repositories, or subscriptions to e-journals and databases, online programs may encourage their students to subscribe to independent virtual libraries such as Questia (http://www.questia.com) and Highbeam (http://www.highbeam.com). Encouraging students to proactively invest in their own access to journal articles gives individuals a distinct advantage over ones who do not have the same level of access to digital information.

*Foreign Dignitaries and Captains of Industry Faculty
The faculty who teach are experts in their fields. The highly prestigious university prides itself on offering courses taught by renowned luminaries in the field. In the past, teaching online was seen as lacking in status, and research by O'Quinn and Corry (2002) listed that as the main detractor. In 2006, perceptions have changed, and the ability to teach individuals who are distributed across the world is considered a way to gain prestige, as well as to share one's life experience with others (Universal Class, 2006).

For example, Pakistan's Ambassador to the United States, Ahmad Kamal, teaches "The United Nations and International Corporations" through DePaul University's School for New Learning (2005) (http://www.snl.info/index.asp). Conducted via video conferencing from the United Nations, the course features video conferencing and asynchronous interaction via e-mail.

*Self-Supporting Financially Viable Business Model
An online university that has achieved prestige within its social group does not have to rely on state support. It will have established profitable online enterprises that will be used to help support some of its programs.

*Program Design
Flexibility, multiple delivery modes, high levels of interaction and support (with faculty, administration, and fellow students), and high quality, up-to-date curriculum and instructional materials form a part of the program design. What differentiates a run-of-the-mill distance program from a prestige program has a great deal to do with the design. The program should be designed in a way that creates conditions in which students learn to think in new ways, apply their knowledge to demonstrate both competence and a deeper understanding by being able to synthesize, problem-solve, innovate, and develop clear, well-

written papers. The program and the design are continually analyzed, reviewed, and updated.

*Committed Faculty and Faculty Support

Even online programs that use only adjunct, part-time faculty must eventually face the fact that in order to achieve and maintain high quality, it is important to have continuity of faculty. If continuity is achieved by means of a core governing faculty board, then it is necessary to meet more than once a year. Ideally, the governing faculty would have activities that keep them engaged with the institution on an ongoing basis. Contact should be made at least once a month, in the form of updates, e-mails, and action items. Discussion board areas should be available for posting ideas, discussing issues, proposing changes, and resolving conflicts.

*Residency options / flexible approach

The prestigious distance education institution of the future may have a bricks and mortar component, although the buildings will be not necessarily be in a single place. Face-to-face residential instructional opportunities will take place throughout the world. Relations will be forged with the ministries of various countries so that, for example, a group could take a class on Mongolian yurts and horse culture. The Mongolian Ministry of the Exterior could host a reception (onsite as well as virtual) and the course would be taken under the auspices of the joint venture – the prestige university and the government. Online components and resources would be offered before, during, and after the face-to-face elements.

*High-quality writing

An online university writing center with extensive resources is available for students. Individuals use it in order to become better writers and to obtain one-on-one mentoring, often available at a very reasonable price, since the writing tutors could be located overseas. In addition, remedial services are also be available.

*Career Placement Services

The prestigious university partners with strong, brand-recognized employment search and mentoring firms. For example, the institution might partner with Monster.com and develop a unique, powerful partnership that would also provide career experience, job openings, and loyal, enthusiastic alumni.

*Internship opportunities
Virtual internships are available where needed. Payment to interns is made as needed, and students receive college credit for their work. The prestige university guides the internship endeavor, and maintains a mindset of partnership and collaboration with the companies and organizations it works with.

*Research – focus on innovation / virtual teams
The prestige university prides itself in high quality instruction, academic counseling and guidance. However, it realizes that the world is not a static place and it endeavors to adapt with the times. By encouraging research and creating the conditions that allow significant innovation to emerge, the run-of-the-mill institution, or, more pointedly, the institution that has been scrambling just to keep its head above waters of change, will pull ahead of the competition. The institution transforms itself into a leading-edge prestige university that is recognized the world over for its innovation, quality, and capacity for far-reaching, inclusive change.

Works Cited and Other Useful Resources

Aboud, S. R. (2005). "Online Education Gets Accolades" *Back to College.* http://www.back2college.com/distancelearning.htm Accessed Jan 6, 2006.

Allen, I. E., & Seaman, J. (2004). *Sizing the Opportunity: The Quality and Extent of Online Education in the United States, 2002 and 2003.* Sloan Consortium. http://www.sloan-c.org/resources/sizing_opportunity.pdf accessed Jan 6, 2006.

American Distance Education Consortium (ADEC). (2005). http://www.adec.edu/ Accessed Jan 3, 2006.

Cornell University. (2005). eCornell. http://www.ecornell.com/ Accessed Jan 5, 2006.

DePaul University School for New Learning. (2005). "The United Nations and International Corporations, Ambassador Kamal." http://www.snl.info/kamal/snl/snlkamal.asp Accessed Jan 5, 2006.

Highbeam.com (2005). Highbeam Library Research. http://www.highbeam.com/Library/ Accessed Jan 6, 2006.

Massachusetts Institute of Technology (2005). MIT Open Courseware Project. http://ocw.mit.edu/index.html Accessed Jan 3, 2006.

O'Quinn, L. & Corry, M. (2004) "Factors the Deter Faculty from Participating in Distance Education" *Online Journal of Distance Learning Administration,* Volume V, NumberIV, Winter 2002. http://www.westga.edu/~distance/ojdla/winter54/Quinn54.htm Accessed Jan. 6, 2006.

Questia.com. (2005). Resources. http://home.universalclass.com/myinterests/teachonline.htm Accessed Jan. 6, 2006.

Sloan Consortium. (2005). *Growing by Degrees: Online Education in the United States, 2005.* http://www.sloan-c.org/resources/growing_by_degrees.pdf. Accessed Jan 6, 2006.

Stanford University. (2005). LOCKKS Program. http://www.diglib.org/preserve/stanfordfinal.html Accessed Jan. 4, 2006.

Thunderbird Garvin School of International Management. (2005). Master's Degree in International Management. http://www.thunderbird.edu/students/degree_prog/mbaim/ Accessed Jan 6, 2006.

UniversalClass. (2006). "How Do I Teach Online?" UniversalClass.com. http://home.universalclass.com/myinterests/teachonline.htm Accessed Jan. 6, 2006.

Webber, T. (2005). "Duke iPod Program to Continue Next Year" *Duke Chronicle.* April 5, 2005. http://www.chronicle.duke.edu/vnews/display.v/ART/2005/04/07/425512a814398 Accessed Jan 4, 2006.

Charismatic Leadership and the E-Learning Organization

If you want to get something done in an organization, get a charismatic leader. Although distributed, situational, transformational, and many other leadership models abound, it is amazing how often the focus reverts to the classic model of a charismatic, larger-than-life individual leading a Pickett's Charge unto the breach. Granted, one hopes for slightly better outcomes, but, the model is worth examining, particularly in the e-learning organization.

Leading change requires courage, vision, and across-the-board buy-in. Transition and change are not easy, even in organizations that trade in change and innovation. Anxiety and tensions abound, and a bureaucratic, "management by committee" approach may cause the organization to flounder. Centralized control is one response to change; radical decentralization is another. In either case, one fairly traditional response to ambiguity is to look for a single charismatic leader to emerge.

According to many scholars and historians, there is definitely a role for the charismatic leader, no matter what the organization. A person with vision and the talent to communicate that vision is indispensable in the initial or start-up phase.

Charismatic leadership gets the program off the ground, and it can be used to promote it and obtain "buy-in" across the organization.

According to most writers on the subject, the charismatic leader:

*Possesses a clear vision.

*Understands the vision now, and how it should unfold in the future.

*Articulates the vision in a manner that captures the imagination of the listeners.

*Inflames the passions of the listeners / followers with a vision of the ideal.

*Makes clear connections between the vision and lives of the listeners, and suggests how their goals, ambitions, and dreams can be realized and their lives materially enhanced by endorsing the goal.

*Leads by example. The charismatic leader adheres to the same tenets that he or she espouses, and shows how to put the concepts into practice. It could be a concrete example of how technology in education has changed his or her life.

*Allow dependency and a certain amount of passivity to occur in the followers, which may result in a suspension of action in order to advance the ideas without interruption.

*Encourages listeners to become followers, and to blur self/identity boundaries and to displace narcissistic ego needs and grandiosity onto the charismatic leader.

*Delineates a mission and communicates it effectively to the followers, who can see how it relates to them.

Inescapable Necessity?
The charismatic leadership style may be indispensable in an e-learning organization in need of rapid change. However, there is definitely a "dark side" to charisma, and not just in doomsday cults and rogue nations.

Does a cult of personality work at all in a network, or in a distributed organization? Much depends on the organizational "glue" that holds the structure together.

Fear is an effective, yet ultimately corrosive, glue. In an organization across a distributed network where members are kept in line through fear and omnipresent surveillance, the leader's face and/or the unifying logo is a constant reminder of coercion and of the needs that are to be met if one adheres to the vision.

Freedom from fear creates longer-lasting bonds. Meeting needs, emotional and physical, and giving individuals the freedom to accomplish their tasks in multiple ways, and using creative approaches is of paramount importance in an organization that seeks to thrive over the long term. Charismatic leaders in a distributed environment often promise that members of the organization will be able to self-regulate and to have a great deal of self-determination. However, if the charismatic leader's promises of security and the satisfaction of emotional and physical needs are not fulfilled, they face backlash and anger.

Problems of Charisma in a Distributed Environment
Charismatic leadership can be problematic in a distributed environment. Some contributing factors include the following:

*Cult of personality can lead to the emergence of factions and rival personalities.

*The charismatic leader requires constant image control and "packaging." The non-verbal, semiotic elements of the message may be harder to control in a distributed environment, where unfortunate (or fortunate, depending on your outlook) juxtapositions may result in a complete undermining of the message.

*Maintaining control requires keeping the vision "hot" and the persuasive elements "fresh." Ethical issues can be sidestepped in the quest for efficacy.

*The locus of control can be too centralized, and the decision-makers can be out of touch with the needs of people / entities in the network.

*There may be an untoward emphasis on affect, which is to say that the charismatic leader may try to maintain a tight grip on the emotions and emotional needs of the followers. The followers may be asked to disregard real physical conditions and the psychological climate and to delay the satisfaction of needs for a better pay-off sometime in the always-nebulous future.

The charismatic leader who practices such coercive tactics will eventually be caught up in a net of cognitive dissonance. In the short run, however, the discomfort may be masked by the followers' willingness to believe in the concept of a necessary sacrifice.

Perhaps, now that we're ending the discussion of charismatic leadership in a distributed environment, in an e-learning organization, it is useful to revisit definitions of charisma.

Charisma derives from the Greek word, *charis,* which means gift. Associated with the notion of gift, are rather superhuman or magical attributes – charm, the power to captivate, the ability to encourage individuals to suspend disbelief.

I'd like to close the discussion of charismatic leadership in an e-learning organization with the suggestion that probably the only effective and ethical use of extreme charisma in such an organization is, most resolutely, *not* to build a cult of personality. It is absolutely inadvisable to construct the notion of charismatic leadership around a single person or persona and then to distribute it in multiple digital forms (podcast, image, logo, emoticon, streaming media) across the network.

The true *charis,* or charming and enrapturing gift, is the Internet itself, and the qualities of the network that bring out the best in the points along the network, the individual participants.

In a truly distributed environment, the charismatic leader is the network itself, with the charm, power to animate hearts, minds, and spirits, and to inspire action, creativity, and constructive thought.

I feel a fit of visionary sci-fi coming on... perhaps I should stop now, and save the discussion of how the network itself becomes a charismatic leader for another day.

Vision and Leadership in the E-Learning Organization

What are defining characteristics of vision in an e-learning organization? With all the talk about vision and mission, are people really taking the time to speculate on what that might look like?

While individuals understand the role of vision in an organization, the importance of vision is even more pronounced in an e-learning organization, where communities of practice include team members who are often separated by time and place, but united by technology.

Characteristics of vision in an e-learning organization can include the following:

Future-based: It is flexible, and attainable in the near future, with long-range goals also in place. It is not too rigid a vision, a dn it accommodates individual differences, locations, technology, and cultures.

Open-ended: A vision open enough for individuals to see themselves in the picture. The desired outcomes involve behaviors that the individual finds appealing and potentially enriching.

Connected: A connection is established between the individual and the leaders who articulates the vision. The result is deep identification with the concept, which leads to an understanding of self, society, and community.

Engaged Affect: It has the capacity to inspire, inflame, and to result in ongoing commitment and persistence in spite of discouraging events.

Tolerance for Frustration: The vision encourages delayed gratification, and provides a mechanism for overcoming frustration.

Collective: The vision encourages individuals to release their individual goals and objectives and to substitute a collective one, where the good of the whole is valued over individual gain.

Creative contribution: The vision inspires one to contribute one's individual, unique talent within a team, and to modify one's skills to adapt oneself to meet the needs of the group, and to achieve the collective goals.

Distributed teams / Virtual collaboration: Individuals see how they fit within the vision, and they contribute their part by means of virtual collaboration in a highly distributed environment.

Articulated in multiple delivery modes: The vision can be articulated and realized by means of multiple modalities, including text, streaming media, audio, graphics, movies.

Collective contributions: Resources -- time, talent, funds, equipment, ideas -- are contributed "any time / any place."

Characteristics of Transformational Leaders in the E-Learning Organization

James McGregor Burns, whose classic works on leadership closely examine the characteristics of the world's great leaders has, after decades of study, concluded that all great leaders have in common a few defining characteristics.

The first, the power to inspire, motivate, and transform, is based on the ability to develop a vision for oneself and one's fellow human beings.

The second, a firm inner commitment to a personal vision, involves the willingness to listen, observe, absorb the anxieties of the times and to be willing to rise to all challenges.

The desire to learn is also the desire for positive transformation, and the ability to transcend the self-limiting attitudes and circumstances that one faces when one least wants or expects it.

James McGregor Burns maintains that leadership involves inspiring and motivating individuals, and thereby persuading them to want to become followers and leaders simultaneously. Vision is the unifying force.

Bernard Bass finds that charismatic leadership inspire and motivate through the force of personality, and that their ability to communicate a vision encourages projection and affiliation.

Manfred Kets de Vries suggests that charismatic leaders convince followers to give up their narcissistic needs and to project them onto the leader. Thus, they are able to make others responsible for their destiny, in the hopes of active transformation where the leader is the instrument, the change agent. Thus, the charismatic leader allows the followers to see the realization of their hopes and dreams.

The desire to learn, the hunger for knowledge needed to implement a vision -- these are the characteristics that define the transformational leader. Leaders in the e-learning organization, with a profound dedication and commitment to the pursuit of knowledge and lifelong learning, must understand that in order to innovate, adapt, and survive, they must exhibit the qualities of great leaders. This involves being able to grasp, define, and articulate the vision in a way that motivates team members in the community of practice to work together.

Distributed Leadership in the E-Learning Organization

Distributed leadership is often referred to as democratic leadership, which gives an indication of the profoundly non-hierarchical nature of power and authority structures in communities of practice or sub-group task forces that are called upon to realize organizational missions and outcomes. It is a powerful organizational strategy, and one that makes excellent use of the resources - human, physical, and financial - of an organization. Because of its usefulness, and overview and discussion are provided below.

Characteristics of Individuals Within an Organization with Distributed Leadership:

Individuals perceive themselves as stakeholders: Because of this perception, all individual team members are willing and able to assume leadership positions, when needed.

The organizational mission can be achieved in stages: The tasks needed to achieve the mission can be broken down into component parts and distributed to the teams best able to achieve the tasks.

Distributed roles and tasks: They take place in different time zones, places, and under widely divergent conditions.

Leaders have expert (rather than title) authority: Leadership shifts according to need; the leader role generally resides with the person who has expert authority for the designated task.

Vision is a unifying force: A clearly articulated vision which is equally shared among all members exerts incredible cohesive force. It is what allows progress to be made without diverging or going off course.

Collaborative teams formed for specific purposes: The teams have fluid membership, which changes according to the task, the roles, and the requisite talent.

Communities of practice emerge: Although collaborative activities tend to disband, the communities of practice maintain their affiliation long after the task, and often connect with each other in order to brainstorm about future needs and potential collaborative configurations.

Aspects of Distributed Leadership (after Woods, 2004) as applied to the e-learning organization

Analytical concepts: The notion of a vision, mission, and desired outcomes constitute an analytical foundation.

Emergent and dispersed: This contrasts with leadership by a single individuals; distributed leadership is characterized by the constant appearance and/or emergence of leaders, which are not necessarily in a single location, but instead, are dispersed in time and geographical space.

Inclusive, based on contingent status: Participation by team members hinges on organizational need and the importance of the vision, mission, and outcomes. Teams and communities of practice are open and inclusive, rather than rigid.

Formally neutral: The individuals are task-oriented, and political or ideological agendas are considered unnecessary and counter-productive.

Instrumental autonomy: Team members are less constrained by existing teams than in an organization in which leadership stays in one location. They are able to act with autonomy when their actions are perceived to help bring the organization to the realization of its goals.

Functional toward human capacities: Leadership shifts according to specific, finite, task-oriented needs. Individuals may assume leadership for the time that their specific skills, talents, or other attributes are needed, and then may abnegate leadership when that moment of need is over.

Although writers on educational leadership tend to propose competing terms for distributed leadership, and alternatively refer to it as dispersed, collaborative, democratic, or shared leadership, all tend to agree that it is the prevailing model in an environment that is employed in organizations that have numerous tasks to accomplish, and a wide variety of skills and resources.

The e-learning organization benefits from a distributed model because it allows collaboration, creative problem-solving, and innovative product design and resources management in an environment that is characterized by rapid technological change, and swiftly emerging learner demands.

Useful References

Barth, R. S. (2001) Learning by Heart, San Francisco, CA: Jossey-Bass.

Burns, J. M. (1978) Leadership, New York: Harper & Row. Castells, M. (1996) The Network Society, Oxford: Blackwell.

Court, M. (2003) Towards democratic leadership. Co-principal initiatives. International Journal of Leadership in Education, 6(2), 161-183.

Fullan, M. (2001) Leading in a Culture of Change. San Francisco, CA: Jossey-Bass.

Gronn, P. (2003) Leadership: who needs it? School Leadership and Management, 23(3), 267-290.

Gronn, P. and Rawlings-Sanaei, F. (2003) Recruiting principals in a climate of disengagement. Australian Journal of Education, 47 (2), 172-184.

Hargreaves, D.H. (1999) The knowledge-creating school, British Journal Education Studies, 47 (2), 122-144. Kets de Vries, M. (1999) High-Performance Teams, Lessons from the Pygmies. Organizational Dynamics, 27 (3), 66-77.

Leithwood, K & Jantzi D. (1990) Transformational leadership: how principal can help reform school cultures, School Effectiveness and School Improvement, 1(4), 249-280.

O'Neill, B. (2002) Distributive Leadership: Meaning Practice (Milton Keynes: The Open University).

Senge, P. (1990) The Fifth Discipline: the art and practice of the learning organization, New York: Doubleday.

Spillane, J. P., Halverson, R., and Diamond, J.B. (2001) Investigating School Leadership Practice: A Distributive Perspective. Educational Researcher, April 2001, pp. 23-28.

Wenger, E. (1998) Communities of Practice, Cambridge: Cambridge University Press.

Woods, P.A. (2004) Democratic leadership: drawing distinctions with distributed leadership. International Journal of Leadership in Education, March 2004, 7(1), 3-26.

Podcasts and e-Learning

Podcast Theory Gap

Online learners seem to prefer using audio and web-based information in ways that counter what researchers recommend.

Although instructional designers do not often like to mention this, the fact is, it is the rare learner who will sit at a computer and willingly watch a 20 or 30-minute presentation.

However, the same learners are happy to listen to an audio file (podcast or book on tape). Although multimedia presentations are not intended to be used in this way, many individuals download the audio aspect separately and listen to it while doing something else, usually something routine: commuting to work, routine data entry on the computer, preparing food in the kitchen, working in the garden.

Later, they will scan through the printout they made. This will be read without the audio.

Do current ideas about working memory and cognitive processing shed any light? What are the implications for developers of online courses, knowing that learners may not be using the media in the environment it was intended?

Fight Audio with Audio: Podcasts and Audio as a Way to Combat Intrusive Thoughts.

"Quiet in the library! Turn off music while you're studying!" Librarians and mothers everywhere utter those words. According to cognitive psychologists who point to the Split Attention Principle and the Coherence Principle, moms and librarians have been right on target. However, millions of computer programmers, writers, students, and artists beg to differ. When they put on headphones and their favorite music, not only do they block out distracting noise which is externally generated, they also help block out intrusive, distracting thoughts that are internally generated. They listen to music as they are reading, as well as when they are doing work that requires intense concentration.

When Retrieving Data, Use Folksonomies and Taxonomies.
Why bother to put anything into short-term memory except the
most basic of cues or mnemonic tags? Furl, google, and
taxonomies will take care of the rest. Unfortunately, many
individuals do not even try to organize knowledge in a
hierarchical way. Instead, they focus on a connectivist approach,
which relies on linking and computer-aided search functions.
The Living Taxonomy Project explores some of these
implications (http://www.livingtaxonomy.org/), as do e-storage
utility programs such as Looksmart's FURL
(http://www.furl.net/index.jsp) and deli.cio.us
(http://del.icio.us/), which utilize "social bookmarks."

What can we make of these habits? How do they relate to
current ideas about working memory and principles used in
instructional design, such as the "Split Attention Principle" and
the "Coherence Principle"?

According to A. D. Baddeley (1986), working memory involves
a multi-phase interaction with cognition, so that humans process
information from their immediate environment, store data about
their past experience, and develop and organizing framework
that will support the acquisition of new knowledge.

The implications for the use of audio in e-learning are multiple.
First, the audio information should make connections to what is
happening in the immediate environment in a way that
reinforces an organizing framework that is being developed.
Second, the content should help establish connections between
past, present, and potential (or future) information so that when
new knowledge is acquired, it is organized in a retrievable way.
In short, the audio should be classifiable into categories, and of
sufficient flexibility to allow cognitive processes to store,
retrieve, and organize information.

According to Baddeley, short-term working memory is limited.
The way the brain process information has to do with the fact
that it has limited capacity in two channels that gather and
process information: the auditory and visual. The "Split
Attention Principle" suggests that one should not overload either
one of the channels, and that the two channels should reinforce
each other.

To put it another way, one should avoid cognitive overload, and audio information should contain clear signals to connect it to the verbal and visual information. Extraneous or distracting auditory information should be avoided, and one should not require the user to require the full text script along with the audio.

This is not to say that it is not useful to have a full-text script available. However, in a presentation, it is better to keep the verbal and visual elements organized in complementary components.

R. E. Mayer and R. Moreno (1999) conducted research that reinforced the idea that cognitive overload is a barrier to learning. According to their findings, an ideal learning environment minimizes or eliminates irrelevant sound / audio. They pointed to the "Split Attention Principle," which states that "students learn better when the instructional material does not require them to split their attention between multiple sources of mutually referring information" (Moreno and Mayer, 2003). Further, all audio should be carefully designed so that it reinforces the message being presented via other media.

The "Coherence Principle" (Moreno and Mayer, 2003), similarly reinforces the importance of avoiding extraneous and/or irrelevant audio. They also discuss the importance of verbal cues and signs.

It bears pointing out that although the findings by cognitive psychologists incorporate models of the brain and brain function that have been recently developed due to new technologies and techniques, they reinforce notions that have been in circulation since Roman times.

Classical rhetoric and oratory contains the same basic concepts as the principles discussed above, and it proposes structure and technique for doing so. Horace (Ars Poetica) applies the concepts to written discourse that would also be presented in oratory. Later, the elocutionary movement in England, which was deeply influenced by classical Greek and Roman texts brought together notions about how the mind makes meaning (deductive and inductive reasoning), and presentation.

George Campbell and Richard Whately were noted in this field. Whately's *Elements of Rhetoric* (1828) and George Campbell's *The Philosophy of Rhetoric* (1841) both deal with how to organize a speech, presentation, or written argument. Their focus on logic privileges ideas about how the mind makes meaning, and where, why, and when the mind latches onto (recognizes), then organizes and processes information.

References and Useful Resources

Baddeley, A.D. (1986) *Working memory.* Oxford, England. Oxford University Press.

Campbell, George. (1841). *The Philosophy of Rhetoric.*

Cicero. *Partitiones Oratoriae.*
http://ccat.sas.upenn.edu/bmcr/2005/2005-04-18.html

Chandler, P. & Sweller, J. (1992). The split-attention effect as a factor in the design of instruction. *British Journal of Educational Psychology, 62*, 233-246.

Craig, C. P. (1985). The Structural Pedigree of Cicero's Speeches Pro Archia, Pro Milone and Pro Quinctio, *CP* 80: 136-37.

Horace. *Ars Poetica.* (The Art of Poetry).
http://www.thelatinlibrary.com/horace/arspoet.shtml

Mayer, R. E. (1997). Multimedia learning: Are we asking the right questions? *Educational Psychologist, 32*, 1-19.

Mayer, R. E. & Anderson, R. B. (1991). Animations need narrations: An experimental test of a dual-coding hypothesis. *Journal of Educational Psychology, 83,* 484-490.

Mayer, R. E. & Anderson, R. B. (1992). The instructive animation: Helping students build connections between words and pictures in multimedia learning. *Journal of Educational Psychology, 84*, 444-452.

Psychology, 90, 312-320.

Mayer, R. E., Moreno, R., Boire M., & Vagge S. (1999). Maximizing constructivist learning from multimedia communications by minimizing cognitive load. *Journal of Educational Psychology , 91*, 638-643.

Moreno, R. & Mayer, R. E. (2000). A coherence effect in multimedia learning: The case for minimizing irrelevant sounds in the design of multimedia instructional messages. *Journal of Educational Psychology, 97*, 117-125.

Moreno, R. & Mayer, R. E. (1999). Cognitive principles of multimedia learning: The role of modality and contiguity. *Journal of Educational Psychology, 91*, 358-368.

Moreno, R. & Mayer, R. E. (2003). A Learner-Centered Approach to Multimedia Explanations: Deriving Instructional Design Principles from Cognitive Theory. http://imej.wfu.edu/articles/2000/2/05/index.asp

Mousavi, S.Y., Low, R., & Sweller, J. (1995). Reducing cognitive load by mixing auditory and visual presentation modes. *Journal of Educational Psychology, 87*, 319-334.
Paivio, A. (1986). *Mental representation: A dual coding approach*. Oxford, England: Oxford University Press.

Sweller, J. (1988). Cognitive load during problem solving: Effects on learning. *Cognitive Science, 12*, 257-285.

Sweller, J., Chandler, P. (1994). Why some material is difficult to learn. *Cognition and Instruction, 12*, 185-233.

Whately, R. (1928). *Elements of Rhetoric*. Mayer, R. E. & Moreno, R. (1998). A split-attention effect in multimedia learning: Evidence for dual processing systems in working memory. *Journal of Educational*

Listening to What Interests You: Podcasts for Effective E-Learning

Podcasts can be used in e-learning to combat intrusive thoughts. They can be a part of an effective self-regulatory strategy which also accommodates multiple learning styles while overcoming intrusive thoughts and the anxiety that accompanies them. As a result, academic performance can improve, while increasing self-concept and self-efficacy.

While the traditional classroom can be a place where learners can engage in conversations, debates, and non-verbal transactions, thus keeping unwanted mental intrusions at bay, the online or distance environment can function in precisely the opposite way and actually create an environment that triggers intrusive thoughts. Social isolation, a lack of engagement with a community of practice, and a highly text-based or visual learning environment leaves the auditory channels unused, and it keeps the individual from being fully engaged with respect to multiple learning styles. Further, any anxiety produced by the isolation, or frustration due to ambiguities in expectations and performance can even trigger unwanted mental intrusions. The undesired thoughts can spark a chain reaction of cause-and-effect responses to the intrusive thoughts as the individual tries to combat them, or feels anxiety about experiencing them.

What are intrusive thoughts, anyway? Intrusive thoughts are unwanted mental intrusions that are often disturbing and result in anxiety. According to the *DSM-IV,* intrusive thoughts or unwanted mental intrusions can be caused by or accompany a number of psychological conditions, including anxiety, obsessive-compulsive disorder, paranoia, grief, post-traumatic stress disorder, and schizophrenia.

However, it is not necessary to have a severe psychological malady to suffer from unwanted mental intrusions. Anything that causes anxiety, including performance anxiety can result in intrusive thoughts. Other intrusive thought triggers include family discord, traumatic incidences, work-related worry, and social pressure.

Strauss (1969) and others suggest that intrusive thoughts (even auditory hallucinations) are a normal psychological phenomenon which fall well within the range of ordinary human experience. Nevertheless, the disturbing nature of the thoughts, coupled with the fact that they are unwanted, lead to negative beliefs about the thoughts (Slade & Bentall, 1988; and Posey & Losch, 1983).

Intrusive thoughts can be exacerbated by negative beliefs about intrusive thoughts, as well as negative beliefs about oneself in response to thoughts. Ironically, thought-control strategies often backfire, and engender or propagate more intrusive thoughts, leading to unwanted intrusive thoughts about the unwanted intrusive thoughts; or "meta-worry" about worrying.

S. Cartwright-Hatton and A. Wells (1987) found that there is a relationship between worry and negative beliefs about intrusive thoughts. This translates to a fear of intrusive thoughts that can be, in essence, paralyzing.

An effective strategy for breaking the cycle of intrusive thoughts is to have a method for intervening, countervailing them with cognitive engagement. The intrusive thoughts can be minimized or eliminated by focusing and maintaining attention on a cognitively engaging activity such as listening to a podcast. Most effective is listening while doing something with one's body in order to bring about kinaesthetic learning as well.

M. Chung etal (2005) found that the number and intensity of intrusive thoughts suffered by those diagnosed with post-traumatic stress disorder (PTSD) is directly related to the intensity of the traumatic incident. Further, they found that the individual's age made no difference in the nature of the intrusive thoughts. Young and elderly alike experienced similar levels of intrusive thoughts, depending on the nature of the traumatic incident that led to the intrusive thoughts. Thus, extremely traumatic events are good predictors of the presence of intrusive thoughts, and it can be assumed that anyone who has experienced violent, traumatizing, disturbing incidences will possess a certain likelihood of having unwanted mental intrusions, regardless of age.

J. Walker and J. Boyce-Tillman (2002) examined the role of focused concentration and auditory channels in self-regulation in cases where children suffered from anxiety. Specifically, they studied the impact of music lessons and whether or not the children were able to develop self-regulatory strategies that involved a combination of auditory and kinaesthetic engagement.

Using podcasts in e-learning can

**spark interest and stimulate connections, which help set up ideal conditions for learning (Gagne's findings on the conditions of learning are helpful).

**help accommodate different learning styles and preferences by providing auditory learners a way to organize meaning. It can be used in conjunction with a physical activity - typing, walking, taking notes - which can help the kinaesthetic learners as well (Gardner and Kolb's theories apply).

**motivate learners by building self-efficacy (Bandura's theories can apply).

**block or replace intrusive thoughts and help assuage anxiety (Deming's findings are very insightful).

**forge connections between an abstract concept and real-life, particularly if the learner is able to listen to the podcast while being in the environment to which the concepts relate. Listen to a podcasts on growing chysanthemums while walking through a greenhouse. Kolb's theories are illuminating.

Finally, for those who have suffered traumatic incidences resulting in anxiety, PTSD, and unwanted mental intrusions, podcasts can be a highly effective strategy -- a godsend -- that gives learners hope when they had just about given up all hope of the transforming power of education.

References and Useful Resources.

Brewin, C. R., Christodoulides, J., & Hutchinson, G. (1996). Intrusive thoughts and intrusive memories in a nonclinical sample. Cognition and Emotion, 10 (10), 107-112.

Cartwright-Hatton, S., & Wells, A. (1997). Beliefs about worry and intrusions: The metacognitions questionnaire and its correlates. Journal of Anxiety Disorders, 11, 279-296.

Chung, M. C., Dennis, I., Easthope, Y., Farmer, S., & Werrett, J. (2005). Differentiating posttraumatic stress between elderly and younger residents. Psychiatry. 68(2), 164-173.

Gaskell, S. L., Wells, A., & Calam, R. (2001). An Experimental investigation of thought suppression and anxiety in children. British Journal of Clinical Psychology, 40, 45-56.

Kember, D., Jenkins, W., & Ng, K.C. (2003). Adult students' perceptions of good teaching as a function of their conceptions of learning -- Part 1. Influencing the development of self-determination. Studies in Continuing Education, 25(2), 239-251.

Kember, D., Jenkins, W., & Ng, K.C. (2004). Adult students' perceptions of good teaching as a function of their conceptions of learning -- Part 2. Implications for the evaluation of teaching. Studies in Continuing Education, 26(1), 81-97.

Kendall, P. C. (1985). Toward a cognitive-behavioural model of child psychopathology and a critique of related interventions. Journal of Abnormal Child Psychology, 13, 357-372.

Kendall, P. C., Chansky, T. E., Kane, M. T., Kim, R. W., Kortlander, E., Conan, K. R., Sessa, F. M., & Siqueland, L. (1992). Anxiety disorders in youth: Cognitive behavioral interventions. Needham Heights, MA: Allyn & Bacon.

Morrison, A.P., Haddock, G., & Tarrier, N. (1995). Intrusive thoughts and auditory hallucinations: A cognitive approach. Behavioural and Cognitive Psychotherapy, 23, 265-302.

Pennebaker, J. W. (1993). Putting stress into words: Health, linguistic, and therapeutic implications. Behavioral Research Therapy, 31, 539-548.

Pennebaker, J. W., & Beall, S. (1986). Confronting a traumatic event: Toward an understanding of inhibition and disease. Journal of Abnormal Psychology, 95, 274-281.

Pennebaker, J., Mayne, T., & Francis, M. (1997). Linguistic predictors of adaptive bereavement. Journal of Personality and Social Psychology, 72, 863-871.

Posey, T. B., & Losch, M. E. (1983). Auditory hallucinations of hearing voices in 375 normal subjects. Imagination, Cognition and Personality, 2, 99-113.

Salkovskis, P. M. (1985). Obsessive-compulsive problems: A cognitive-behavioural analysis. Behaviour Research and Therapy, 23, 571-583.

Sarason, I. G. (1984). Stress, anxiety and cognitive interference: reactions to tests. Journal of Personality and Social Psychology, 46, 929-938.

Sarason, I. G. (1988). Anxiety, self-preoccupation and attention. Anxiety Research, 1, 3-7.

Sarason, I. G., Sarson, B. R., and Pierce, G. R. (1990). Anxiety, cognitive interference, and performance. Journal of Social Behavior and Perosnality, 5, 1 – 18.

Slade, P. D., & Bentall, R. P. (1988). Sensory deception: A scientific analysis of hallucination. London: Croom Helm.

Smith, B., & Caputi, P. (2001). Cognitive interference in computer anxiety. Behavior & Information Technology, 20 (4), 265-273.

Smyth, J., & Pennebaker, J. (1999). Telling one's story: Translating emotional experiences into words as a coping tool. In C. R. Snyder (Ed.), Coping: The psychology of what works (pp. 70-89). New York: Oxford University Press.

Smyth, J., True, N., & Souto, J. (2001). Effects of writing about traumatic experiences: The necessity for narrative structuring, Journal of Social and Clinical Psychology, 20 (2), 161-172.

Stewart, S. H., Conrod, P. J., Gignac, M. L., & Pihl, R. O. (1998). Selective processing biases in anxiety-sensitive men and women. Cognition and Emotion, 12 (1), 105-133.

Strauss, J. S. (1969). Hallucinations and delusions as points on continua function: Rating scale evidence. Archives of General Psychiatry, 21, 581-586.

Walker, J., & Boyce-Tillman, J. (2002). Music lessons on prescription? The impact of music lessons for children with chronic anxiety problems. Health Education, 102 (4), 172-179.

Podcasts and Working Memory: A Breakthrough for E-Learning?

The problem with podcasts in e-learning, claim nay-sayers, is precisely the aspect that makes it so popular: mobility and the ability to download and listen in any place or time, unleashed from the laptop or desktop computer. They claim that learners will tend to listen "out of context" and thus will be unable to organize the information properly when not surrounded by relevant content or visual cues to reinforce the information. Thus, in the absence of strong, external organizing cues (visual, primarily), the information delivered via audio file is reduced to "noise." According to this negative portrayal of learning via podcast, the information that has been delivered is useless because it is not retrievable.

Those who maintain that one should never listen to course content away from a classroom or a rich, visual cue-laden e-learning space tend to be fans of multimedia powerpoint presentations, and visual presentations synched with audio. To a certain extent, the naysayers have a point, because they are, at the very least, accommodating multiple learning styles. The problem, however, is that presentations organized in this way tend to encourage passive listening, and little or no active, or participatory, listening.

However, to focus simply on learning styles, and to attempt to always link audio with powerpoints or other visual multimedia tends to discount or overlook altogether the role of working memory, and the ability of cognitive systems to interact with aural stimuli and incoming content. Working memory can function to organize, process, tag, and file information for future retrieval.

Working memory functions to allow the individual to keep steps of a process or categories in mind so that information can be "tagged" for retrieval. Other process-related uses of the working memory can be to help keep the mind on task, in the sense that it can help bring in or activate helpful relevant information (categories, relevant experiences) and block or screen out irrelevant information and distractors.

Description and Processes of Working Memory

Short-term memory is often misunderstood, and individuals fail to recognize that it is a part of a complex cognitive system.

A clear definition of short-term memory is provided by Baddeley and Hitch (1974), who explain that it is not a single storage mechanism of limited capacity. Instead, it consists of three elements or sub-processes, which include two ancillary support transfer systems, a phonological loop (audio repeated, either in the mind or externally), and a visuospatial sketchpad (in memory).

This cognitive system contains a "central executive" which exerts control over the processes, and assures that the order of functioning leads to repeatable transfer of data, and functions that deliver chunks of content in a way that allows them to fit nicely into a larger structure.

Other investigators such as Hambrick and Engle (2002) have found that working memory is most successful when it keeps task-relevant information in a highly activated and accessible state, and screens or blocks information that is irrelevant to the task. Further, working memory can time-release relevant information that facilitates the tagging of information so that it is retrieved in a way that conforms with desired outcomes.

It can be said that it is possible for the working memory to transport the information to the "central executive" in a chaotic manner. However, if the information that is being presented contains verbal cues that trigger the "phonological loop," and there is some awareness of how and why knowledge would be organized in a certain way, then the working memory can effectively keep knowledge systems well organized.

The "phonological loop," which is often seen in action as children read aloud, or individuals speak the knowledge, contains cues and repetitions. These are "breathing spaces" that help the learners stop, pause, and organize before moving on.

The phonological loop is a vital part of the cognitive process. The next step is the working memory's "visuospatial sketchpad" (Baddeley and Hitch), which transports a mental image. If the information is in the form of a podcast, which is to say an audio file, then the spoken word (or sound) triggers a particular image.

Relevance of Working Memory in Processing Information for Learning via Podcasts

Skillful audio file creators will construct their stories so that they connect with specific items in other parts of the memory in order to make meaning and to be retrievable. For example, aural cues may connect to specific shared experiences, or may refer to a scene or a place that is likely to be understood by the audience. Needless to say, to be able to develop an audio broadcast that is remembered in a uniform way, where the listeners draw similar conclusions, requires a very good understanding of one's audience, their values, experience, and background.

Developing effective and memorable audio also relies on the possibility of having visual cues or texts on hand as supplements, in order to guide the learners in organizing knowledge in cognitive pathways developed by the instructor and in line with the ultimate learning goals and outcomes of the course.

Working Memory, Podcasts and E-Learning in Real-Life Situations

Jhahendra likes to listen to audio files on her mp3 player as she commutes to her job, roughly an hour on the subway, and then the train. The train is often crowded, and sometimes there is no place to sit, so she is forced to stand. Jhahendra enjoys listening because it allows her to mentally escape the cacophony. At the same time, she realizes that it is not a complete escape. There are intrusive and distracting events, such as when commuters jostle her and jockey for position. Her professor said it seems counterproductive to him for her to listen to audio files away from the powerpoint. After all, he said, she will not have any idea how to organize the knowledge. Jhahendra disagrees. She says that she remembers the points quite well, particularly since the lecture involves small chunks of information that are clearly marked in terms of content and theme. Jhahendra assured him that listening is productive rather than destructive. By the time she sits down with the Powerpoint, she is familiar with the concepts. The audio has paved the way to deeper understanding.

Karlston listens to podcasts on his iPod mini as he goes on a 45-minute gauntlet of walking and running. He does it four times a week, and he pushes himself fairly hard. He finds that he tends to have gaps in his recollection of the podcasts during the time he is in pain or panting from pushing himself up a hill in 95-degree weather. "Maybe you need a treadmill for total recall," joked his professor, Dr. Anchorite Kempe. Karlston realized it was a joke, but he wondered if there was something to kinaesthetic memory. As a test, he decided to alternate days for listening to podcasts, just to see if the podcast from the day before would appear in his working memory after getting the kinaesthic cue, when physical conditions replicated the day before. While he hated the notion that it was very possible that cognitively he functioned in the ways that the behaviorists suggested, Karlton was intrigued by the fact that he did in fact tend to recall things when in similar settings. He decided to listen to podcasts in settings that resembled the room where he would take comprehensive exams, and when he read the texts, he muttered phrases from the podcasts under his breath. His mother suggested that he see a psychiatrist and his girlfriend started to look at him in a strange way. He aced his comprehensive exams, though.

Recommendations

For maximum learning effectiveness, one can use podcasts in the following ways to harness the power of working memory and avoid some of the pitfalls of over-reliance on short-term memory.

**Make the text from podcasts available, and encourage learners to read the texts either before or after listening to the podcasts, but not during the listening experience.

**Encourage listeners to create outlines based on what they are listening to. Note-taking can take place while they are listening, or immediately afterwards (if it is unsafe to write while listening).

**Use podcasts to combat unwanted intrusive thoughts, and use them as a strategy for maintaining attention.

**Avoid bland podcasts that are not punctuated by "trigger words" or cues that will connect to a structure recognized by the learners' "central executive" after the content has been transferred via working memory.

References and Useful Resources.

Baddeley, A. D, Elridge, M., & Lewis, V. (1981). The role of subvocalization in reading. *Quarterly Journal of Experimental Psychology: Human Experimental Psychology. 33A,* 439-454.

Baddeley, A. D., & Hitch, G. J. (1974). Working memory. In G. H. Bower (Ed.), *The psychology of learning and motivation* (Vol. 8, pp. 47-89). New York: Academic Press.

Cowan, N. (1995). *Attention and memory: An integrated framework.* Oxford: Oxford University Press.

Daneman, M., and Carpenter, P. A. (1980). Individual differences in working memory and reading. *Journal of Verbal Learning and Verbal Behavior, 19,* 450-466.

Hambrick, D. Z., & Engle, R. W. (2002). Effects of domain knowledge, working memory capacity, and age on cognitive performance. *Cognitive Psychology, 44,* 339-387.

Kahneman, D. (1973). *Attention and effort.* Englewood Cliffs, NJ: Prentice-Hall.

Kane, M. J., Bleckley, M. K., Conway, A. R. A., & Engle, R. W. (2001). A controlled attention view of working memory capacity. *Journal of Experimental Psychology: General,* 130, 169-183.

Moray, N. (1959). Attention in dichotic listening: Affective cues and the influence of instructions. *Quarterly Journal of Experimental Psychology, 11,* 56-60.

Rosen, V.M., & Engle, R. W. (1997). The role of working memory capacity in retrieval. *Journal of Experimental Psychology: General, 126,* 211-227.

Shah, P., & Miyake, A. (1999). Models of working memory: An introduction. In A. Miyake & P. Shah (eds.), *Models of working memory: Mechanisms of active maintenance and executive control* (pp. 1-27). Cambridge, UK: Cambridge University Press.

Zacks, R. T., Hasher, L., & Li, K. Z. H. (2000). Human memory. In T. A. Salthouse & F. I. M. Craik (Eds.), *The handbook of aging and cognition* (2nd ed., pp. 293-357).

Learning and Teaching Strategies that Work

Learning Strategies Applied to Online Courses

Effective design and instruction of distance courses can provide additional support for students who are at risk of failure due to the fact that they never developed effective learning strategies in traditional face-to-face environments.

The problems can be compounded in online and/or hybrid courses, where more self-regulation is required and where social or group behaviors are not automatic sources of support, reinforcement, and cognition-building.

Such problems, however, present an opportunity for online and hybrid course developers to create courses that guide students in the mastery of effective learning strategies, and equip them with an array of tactics for successfully negotiating not only the particular course, but also learning in general. The design can function as non-obtrusive virtual coaching, with strategies and approaches that can be emulated by others and applied to other learning situations and settings.

In 1996, H. Tait and N. J. Entwistle published the results of a study that explored the connection between ineffective study habits and academic success, and it suggested that poor study habits and learning strategies place a student at risk. While this may seem self-evident, the study revealed very useful connections between behavioral, cognitive, and emotional strategies.

The authors, Tait and Entwistle, concluded that the most effective learning strategies were ones that reinforced each other in a seamless, integrative manner. These insights are very useful for designers, instructors, and administrators who can develop and guide courses in ways that can naturally incorporate the acquisition of learning strategies.

In fact, a well-designed online or hybrid course can (and probably should) teach learning strategies as well as the course content. Needless to say, achieving learning outcomes requires one to have at least some facility with multiple learning strategies, particularly when learning styles differ.

Further, external factors such as lack of access and confusion can create anxiety, frustration, or confusion and can act as barriers to persistence.

Cognitive Learning Strategies

1---Rehearsal

These are procedures used by the student to repeat to himself or herself the course content. In a traditional setting, students often copy notes, or recopy the content. Studies have suggested that this is not particularly effective at achieving deep learning, but it does help students in classification and identification of content.

In an online environment, "rehearsal" is an automatic, and can be built into navigation tools, and reinforced by using color, typography, and design. Learning activities can also ask students to type categories and to rehearse knowledge. This approach is most effective when it requires students to make connections or to classify and organize content.

2---Organization

These are procedures that help students identify key topics and issues, and to build cognitive structures that allow classification, grouping, and inter-relation. It requires synthesis, evaluation, and higher-level activities which can lead to deeper learning.

In an online environment, if students are required to engage in an instructional activity that requires both rehearsal and organization, they are more able to be flexible in their thinking and to use the information in more than one setting or context.

3---Elaboration

This procedure is deeply constructivist in its epistemological underpinnings, which is to say that it requires students to not only repeat, restate, classify, organize, it requires the learner to make connections between disparate chunks of information. It may also require making connections between course content and the learner's own knowledge or experience.

An online course can require students to write essays, or provide brief analyses that require the learner to engage in elaboration. To be most effective, a set of procedures or "guiding questions" can provide the scaffolding needed. Modeling elaboration by providing examples of "situated learning" -- learning that places the content within a certain context and asks the student to transform it -- can lead to the acquisition of effective learning strategies.

Behavioral Learning Strategies

1---Interpersonal help-seeking

In a classroom setting or traditional face-to-face environment, in-class group work or study groups outside the class provide an easy way to seek help.

In an online class, attempts to provide this are multiple, but of highly variable efficacy. The ubiquitous "FAQ" page is useful, but only if there is a good search tool and the student knows what he or she should be asking. A live "help desk" is useful, but usually not class-specific enough to be of much use. Synchronous chat rooms can be helpful, as are opportunities to communicate through internet telephony, such as Skype. Discussion boards can be effective in seeking help, although they tend to be public and postings can be subject to misinterpretation.

2---Interaction / social reinforcement

Interactivity in a face-to-face setting is often most effective when a facilitator moderates discussions and models the behavior that is deemed desirable.

In the online environment, chat and discussion areas can be very effective, particularly if there are multimedia aspects -- video and audio -- that are easily accessed.

Blogs, collaborative projects and games can be ways of modeling positive interaction, and one can "reality check" one's ideas and/or thoughts. One of the most effective methods of achieving social reinforcement in an online environment is to ask students to post a project or paper in order to allow others to see what they are doing and to comment.

3---Seeking help from written material

This strategy involves procedures for obtaining information from books, digital resources, and other items. Key strategies involve teaching how to narrow a search, how to recognize the correct information once it has been retrieved, and how to apply it in an appropriate manner.

The online environment offers many opportunities to coach students on how to retrieve and use information. This can range from the use of a virtual library, or the use of learning objects.

In fact, this is one of the best places for learning objects. Small, highly granular objects -- interactive maps, online dictionaries, diagrams, guides and flowcharts -- can be quite helpful. They can also link with cognitive strategies that involve making connections, organizing, and repeating.

4---Practical application

These procedures ask individuals to try things in the real world. Effective learning strategies can be modeled and transferred by using simulations, games, and virtual worlds.

Self-Regulation Strategies

1---Time management

This is a learning strategy / self-regulation technique that is very difficult to teach and implement in the online environment due to the fact that there are huge distractors lying at one's fingertips.

Timed deadlines, and disabling/disabling access to Instant Messanger, chat, internet telephony, internet, and games may help.

2---Emotional control (anxiety and concentration)

Effective learning strategies in this area include procedures for minimizing and reducing anxiety, lack of concentration, and frustration.

Because of the nature of technology, the online environment can, at times, create anxiety and frustration, particularly when there are technical difficulties and access is interrupted. Poor design and navigation can create anxiety, while good design, navigation, support, and instructional activities can help the learner gain an enhanced sense of self-efficacy and self concept.

3---Motivation

Part of the face-to-face instructional environment includes procedures to motivate individuals who are not interested in the material, or who do not like the instructional environment.

Good instructional design can be very effective in motivating students, or teaching them how to motivate themselves by adding interest, making connections and points of reference to their lives, establishing relevance, and instilling a sense of the usefulness and even urgency in mastering the topic.

4---Comprehension monitoring

In the traditional environment, these refer to procedures that assess the degree to which learning objectives have been attained, and they help the instructor identify where gaps in learning exist.

In the online environment, the successful student has methods of testing, tracking, and checking his or her comprehension of the content and mastery of learning objectives. This often takes the form of e-mailing the instructor to obtain feedback. However, it can also be automated, and students can take online quizzes and/or engage in activities that help them assess whether or not they are on track.

Conclusions

At the risk of seeming to simply parrot the same old thing all the time, what this study reveals is the importance of planning.

Planning an online course so that it helps guide students in the acquisition of effective learning strategies is a multi-pronged endeavor.

It requires a thorough understanding of a) the students, their abilities, backgrounds, language, contexts, beliefs, core values, and reasons for taking the course; b) the technological environment, which includes access, hardware, variability of access, complexity of interface, etc.; c) the kinds of learning objectives that the course of study will generally involve; d) the instructors, their backgrounds and technical ability, their understanding of effective mentoring, and their willingness to adapt to ever-changing technological requirements.

Useful Resources

Ackerman, P. L., Sternberg, R. J., and Glaser, R. (Eds.) (1989). *Learning and individual differences.* New York : Freeman.

Caverly, D. C., and Orlando, V. P. (1991). Textbook Study Strategies. In R. F. Flippo and D. C. Caverly (Eds.), *Teaching reading and study strategies at the college level.* (pp. 86-155). Newark , DE : International Reading Association.

Driskell, J. E., Copper, C., and Moran, A. (1994). Does mental practice enhance performance? *Journal of Applied Psychology,* 78, 805-814.

Schmeck, R. R. (Ed.) (1988). *Learning strategies and learning styles.* New York : Plenum Press.

Tait, H. and Entwistle, N. J. (1996). "Identifying students at risk through ineefcitve study strategies", *Higher Education* 31, 97-116.

Weinstein, C. E., & Mayer, R. E. (1986). The teaching of learning strategies. In M. C. Wittock (Ed.), *Handbook of research on teaching* (3 rd ed. Pp 315-327). New York , Macmillan.

Goal-Setting and Self-Regulation in Online Courses: The Basics

Goal-setting, which is an aspect of self-regulation, can be a vital part of an adult student's success in online learning. It increases motivation dramatically, not only by building in rewards, but also by increasing skill levels and perceived self-efficacy.

In 1979, Locke and Latham published a landmark paper that presented their research on self-regulation and motivation, which involved logging industry workers in the American South and the West. The findings suggested that when individuals are able to set their own goals, and if they are provided the support and resources they need to achieve the goals, productivity increases. This article proposes a goal-setting model that includes the following components: input sources, achieving goal commitment, overcoming resistance to goal acceptance, goal attributes, support elements, and performance. Benefits include high performance, role clarity, and pride in achievement. It also identifies possible dangers of implementing goal-setting. Employees may become dissatisfied by the failures, may be tempted to take short cuts, and may ignore non-goal areas.

Later, Locke and Latham published research that established connections between goal-setting, self-regulation and job satisfaction. It grew out of Locke and Latham's original research, as well as from the Wurzburg school on intention, task and set, Lewin on aspiration, and Ryan on intentions. The results are that goal specificity is key to developing motivating goals. Commitment to goals is also seen as a key element if performance is to be impacted in a positive way. The connections between goal-setting and work satisfaction are revealed to have a direct connection to expectancy theory. High expectancy and specific, high goals will lead to satisfaction when mediating mechanisms such as effort, persistence, direction, and plans lead to contingent and non-contingent rewards.

Further building on earlier research, White developed an evaluation instrument designed to determine how goal-setting relates to the actual performance of university students. The instrument measured the both the goal-setting attitudes and behaviors. Findings found correlations between specific and clear short-term goal-setting and academic performance.

Definitions and Key Concepts

Self-regulation is the way an individual monitors, controls, and directs aspects of his or her cognitive processes and behavior for themselves.

Self-regulation involves the following cognitive processes:

1. Planning: organized steps, includes goal-setting, developing a strategy, and identifying obstacles;
2. Monitoring: involves the ability to observe, acknowledge, and measure progress toward one's objectives;
3. Evaluating: involves assessing outcomes, gauging progress;
4. Reinforcing: reflection and recognition of success, involves reward.

Goal-setting involves self-regulation and is very task and outcome-oriented. It also requires one to develop cognitive abilities and skills.

Application to Adult Online Learners

Self-regulation: Adult learners are beneficiaries of self-regulation because it allows them to create order out of an often chaotic existence, and it helps them organize time, energies, and resources. This is a vital element as adults seek to balance career, family, travel, goals, dreams, and responsibilities.

The following are steps that will help the adult learner build skills needed for self-regulation:

1. Planning.
Set goals => must identify goals
Develop a strategy => analyze the task, describe the desired outcome

Prior experience and knowledge => identify useful knowledge or experience

2. Monitoring
Determine progress => observe and measure
Fine-tuning => identify needed adjustments
Re-assess desired outcomes => Propose changes in order to attain goal

3. Evaluating
Assess strategy => was desired outcome achieved? was it done easily? efficiently?
Lessons learned => Is there anything to modify or incorporate in future attempts?

Goal-Setting:
One of the most widely used approaches to goal-setting is the SMART model, which was developed and popularized by Stephen Covey. The SMART model below includes adaptations for adult learners.

S = Specific - Make the goal very specific, both in terms of time and tasks
M = Measurable - Monitor progress, and recognize when the goals have been achieved
A = Achievable - Impossible goals are very demotivating
R = Resourced - Adult students should always invest in resources needed
T = Time-based - Realistic time frames, with short-term and long-term goals

Useful Articles

Assor, A., Kaplan, H, & Roth, G. (2002). Choice is good, but relevance is excellent: Autonomy-enhancing and suppressing teacher behaviors predicting students' engagement in schoolwork. British Journal of Educational Psychology, 72, 261-278.

This article reports the results of a study to determine how teacher behavior, and self-regulation affects the level to which students engage in their schoolwork. The findings suggested that teachers who were able to explain the relevance of the schoolwork to the students and to model self-regulation had more success in encouraging students to engage with the schoolwork.

Bandura, A. (1997). Self-efficacy: The exercise of control. New York: Freeman.

Boekaerts, M., Pintrich, P. R., & Zeidner, M. (Eds.) (2000). Handbook of self-regulation. San Diego: Academic Press.

Dweck, C. S. (1999). Self-theories: Their role in motivation, personality, and development. Philadelphia: Taylor & Francis.

Locke, E. A., & Latham, G. P. (1990). A theory of goal setting and task performance. Englewood Cliffs, NJ: Prentice Hall.

Locke, E. A., & Latham, G. P. (2002). Building a practically useful theory of goal setting and task motivation: A 35-year odyssey. American Psychologist. 57, 701-717.

Locke E A, Saari L M, Shaw K N & Latham G P. (1981) Goal setting and task performance: 1969-1980. Psychol. Bull. 90, 125-52.

Locke, E. A., & Latham, G. P (1979). Goal setting – A motivational technique that works. Organizational Dynamics, Autumn 1979, 68-80.

Locke, E. A., & Latham, G. P. (1990). Work motivation and satisfaction: Light at the end of the tunnel. Psychological Science, 1, 240-246.

Pervin, L.A. (1992). The rational mind and the problem of volition. Psychological Science, 3, 162-164.

Schunk, D. H. (1995). Self-efficacy and education and instruction. In J. E. Maddux (Ed.), Self-efficacy, adaptation, and adjustment: Theory, research, and application (pp. 281-303). New York: Plenum Press.

Schunk, D. H., & Zimmerman, B. J. (1997). Social origins of

self-regulatory competence. Educational Psychologist, 32, 195-208.

White, F. (2002). A cognitive-behavioural measure of student goal setting in a tertiary educational context. Educational Pscyhology, 22, 285-304.

Zimmerman, B. J. (1998). Developing self-fulfilling cycles of academic regulation: An analysis of exemplary instructional models. In D. H. Schunk & B. J. Zimmerman (Eds.), Self-regulated learning: From teaching to self-reflective practice (pp. 1-19). New York: Guilford Press.

Zimmerman, B. J. (2000). Attaining self-regulation: A social cognitive perspective. In M. Boekaerts, P. R. Pintrich, & M. Zeidner (Eds.), Handbook of self-regulation (pp. 13-39). San Diego: Academic Press.

Rehearsal and Repetition May Be Bad for Learning: Learning Strategies That Work

Rehearsal and repetition may be bad for learning. They are even worse for learners at a distance for whom external influences such as work stress, frequent travel, deployment to war zones, and personal or family issues are creating learning anxiety. This is the conclusion reached by several learning specialists and educational psychologists who studied why students perform poorly even after adhering closely to the "practice makes perfect" traditional cognitive learning strategies of rehearsal, organization, and elaboration.

Ironically, instead of helping students perform, rehearsal and repetition may have negative impacts on performance, as well as self-concept. Unfortunately, in this case, the learning strategies actually exacerbates learning anxiety, and worsens the learner's ability to succeed. Not surprisingly, once a distance learner gets caught in the twin trap of situational anxiety and performance anxiety (heightened by negative self concept and insecurity about learning in general), it is very likely that he or she will not finish the course, and may even drop out of the degree or certificate program.

There are several reasons why rehearsal and repetition are the wrong learning strategy choices for an individual suffering from situational or performance anxiety:

Concentration is required for rehearsal and repetition:
According to some educational psychologists (Kuhl, 1992), people have finite resources for cognitive and information processing. If too much capacity is dedicated to quelling one's anxiety by self-reassurance and relaxation techniques, there is little capacity left for the actual task at hand.

Further, if the learning situation or setting creates distractions, more cognitive resources will be required to maintain focus.

Finally, if an individual is suffering from post-traumatic stress disorder or there are work or family conflicts, unwanted intrusive thoughts may create even more problems with concentration, and require the marshalling of cognitive resources.

Online rehearsal and repetition often take the form of automated, interactive forms, requiring good online access and time online: Many online courses rely heavily on automated, online quizzes and "skill and drill" activities.

While these are considered effective by some, particularly if the test is in the same format, there are questions about the efficacy of skill-and-drill in the attainment of deeper learning.

Nevertheless, this is a moot point for an individual learner who cannot access the quizzes or review materials because he or she has limited access to the Internet, and may be accessing the learning activities through a very slow dial-up connection or wifi node. Needless to say, the frustration involved when one cannot access the material contributes to learner anxiety.

Motivational control lacking as boredom sets in: Motivation is an important factor in success, and anxiety acts as a huge demotivator. Further, learners may find that rehearsal and repetition -- particularly in isolation, is extremely boring. Educational psychologists (Pintrich and DeGroot, 1990), have traced connections between motivation and learning strategies.

Material is too compartmentalized, content too granular, and made irrelevant to real life: Skill and drill activities involving rehearsal, and repetition are, while very labor-intensive and expensive to develop, very attractive to computer-based training and online learning activities designers. The content has fine granularity and can be reused and redeployed in many settings and under many conditions. Further, it's a scalable way to provide instructional activities. However, all the assumptions used to support using skill-and-drill automated activities must be re-examined when learners are in hostile conditions, have little online access, and are working in isolation.

Material must be made relevant, and reconnected to real life. Further, if repetition and rehearsal are used as learning strategies, it must be made clear to the learner that the content forms an foundational underpinning for situated learning to come in the future.

Effective rehearsal and repetition occurs in groups, where immediate support is available: Although it was not mentioned in the studies, one can surmise that traditional on-campus students have formed study groups, or are required to go to lab and discuss the course material. It might be useful to examine if rehearsal, organization, and elaboration are most effective in study groups and informal communities of practice. In distance settings, collaborative strategies rarely involve the cognitive strategies, but instead tend to stress practical application focused around a set of clearly defined outcomes.

Self-Regulatory Strategies Are Critical for Online Students

Researchers (Warr and Downing, 2000) have suggested that self-regulatory learning strategies are the most effective for students suffering from learning anxiety.

Their findings can be applied to online learning as well, particularly when self-regulation (control of emotions, etc.) is combined with behavioral and cognitive learning strategies for an eclectic approach.

Motivation control: Alleviating boredom and maintaining interest by building in rewards and positive reinforcement are quite effective in an online environment. The learner who is suffering from anxiety may feel motivated to persist in the studies if the instructor provides prompt and meaningful feedback, group activities help provide a sense of connection and community, and the course content is clearly relevant to the learner's academic, life, and personal goals.

Help-Seeking and informal study group development: Learner anxiety is augmented by frustration. Frustration can result from technical difficulties, connectivity, unclear interfaces and instructions, and ambiguous performance expectations. A responsive help desk is important, as well as a robust Frequently Asked Questions page. In addition, if possible, establish an onsite mentor or team-leader if several individuals who are taking the course are in the same place of employment or military unit.

Written help-seeking: If learners are aware that they can send e-mails to more than one person, is it very helpful. Although many online programs rely on a queued approach to inquiries to the help desk, with task-sharing, it is also useful to add a personal touch to what can be a very dehumanized elearning space. Anxiety can be exacerbated by seeking help from a faceless entity known only through the design on a computer screen. Personalizing help-seeking helps assuage anxiety.

Practical application: Learning strategies that situate the content and make connections between the content and the individual learner's lived experience are highly effective. This utilizes a constructivist epistemology and my require a rethinking and recasting of learning activities and assessment. Further, a cognitive epistemology comes into play when the individual learner makes connections, and then begins to form categories and to organize the knowledge in systems useful to the learner. Retrieval and application of information are facilitated, and the function is fluid, seamless, and meaningful when the learner can apply the knowledge to a real-life situation, or to solve a problem perceived by the learner to be urgent and relevant.

One useful benefit of using practical application as a learning strategy for students suffering from learning anxiety (whether situational or performance-related), is that the learner can employ the new learning model to other aspects of his or her life. It is more than self-regulation, and more of an eclectic approach to learning and life.

Useful Resources

Driskell, J. E., Copper, C., and Moran, A. (1994). Does mental practice enhance performance? *Journal of Applied Psychology, 78,* 805-814.

Ferguson-Hessler, M. G. M., and de Jong, T. (1990). Studying physics texts: Differences in study processes between good and poor performers. *Cognition and Instruction, 7,* 41-54.

Karabenick, S. A., and Knapp, J. R. (1991). Relationship of academic help seeking to the use of learning strategies and other instrumental achievement behaviors in college students. *Journal of Educational Psychology. 16.* 117-138.

Kuhl, J. (1992). A theory of self-regulation: Action versus state orientation, self-discrimination, and some applications. *Applied Psychology: An International Review, 41,* 97-129.

Mueller, J. H. (1992) Anxiety and performance. In A. P. Smith and D. M. Jones (Eds.), *Handbook of human performance* (Vol 3, pp. 127-160). London : Academic Press.

Pintrich, P. R., and De Groot, E. V. (1990). Motivational and self-regulated learning components of classroom academic performance. *Journal of Educational Psychology, 82.* 33-40.

Seipp, B. (1991). Anxiety and academic performance. A meta-analysis of findings. *Anxiety Research, 4,* 27-41.

Snow, R. E. and Swanson, J. (1992). Instructional psychology -- Aptitude, adaptation, and assessment. *Annual Review of Psychology, 43,* 49.

Warr, P., and Downing, J. (2000). Learning strategies, learning anxiety, and knowledge acquisition. *British Journal of Psychology , 91,* 311-333.

Weinstein, C. E., and Mayer, R. E. (1986). The teaching of learning strategies. In M. C. Wittock (Ed.), *Handbook of research on teaching* (3 rd ed. pp. 315-327). New York , Macmillan.

Text Representation and Cognitive Processes: How the Mind Makes Meaning in e-Learning

Since e-learning relies still relies heavily on text-based learning, it is very helpful to have a basic idea of how the mind makes meaning from discourse. Understanding how the various forms of textual representation operate will help one design more effective instructional materials, activities, and assessments.

According to discourse theorists, written language has the following aspects or components in the text itself, which consist of Surface Code, Textbase, and Situated Text.

It also helps to understand the factors that influence how an individual processes that language. Finally, the mechanisms used for comprehension matter a great deal when one is trying to achieve uniform learning outcomes.

Achieving standard outcomes is simply not possible without first understanding how when and how to activate relevant knowledge, and then how to guide the learner so that he/she acquires skill in selecting the correct meaning-making processes.

Regurgitation? Look to Surface Code.

Surface Code. Surface Code preserves and presents the exact wording and syntactical structure of the discourse.

*Surface code is rarely remembered more than a few minutes.
*To remember surface code, the individual must rehearse, '''repeat, recycle verbatim the text that has been read or identified by its visual appearance. This is often done by means of verbal repetition. The ability to repeat the words does not have any relation whatsoever with comprehension.
*Implications: Avoid quizzes that require verbatim repetition; or, alternatively, when asking students to memorize lists, make certain they are used later as the foundation of categories or classification schemes.

Language Bridges and Glue: Textbase

Textbase. Textbase is made up of propositions that construct "the representation of a particular event, action, state or goal expressed in the text." It consists of predicates (action) and arguments (subject).

The function of textbase is basically twofold, and involves the following two activities:

*help comprehend events, action, etc.
*help link other propositions and force connections, relations, hierarchies

If one thinks of textbase as what glues things together, or what creates bridges from one to another, it makes it perhaps a bit easier to conceptualize the best way(s) to develop instructional materials.

Effective instructional activities could include having students accurately identify the relationships of content (true-false, multiple-choice are useful for this), and to create maps of how the conceptual bridges work (and where they go).

For example, causal relationships, compare-contrast, and extended definitions can help students understand the relations, not just with textbase, but also in more complex aspects, described later.

The connection to life, experience, reality: Situated Text

Situated Text. Situation Model (mental model) is the nonlinguistic, referential context of what the text is about" (Graesser, Singer, Trabasso, 1994).

This is where the student applies his or her knowledge of the world to the content. It is also where the instructional activities should map relationships between the content and the outside / external world. This can be done by providing background and history, by taking an interdisciplinary approach, and by incorporating activities to build deeper understanding.

*Interactions and connections between prior world experience and the surface code and textbase
* Critical in e-learning because it forms the foundation of future learning.
*Implications: Develop readings and instructional materials rich in potential connections with lived experience, and maximize resonances.   Also, be sure to incorporate essays that build deeper connections and which situate meaning. This includes compare-contrast, extended definition, process, causality, and argumentation.

Levels of Discourse: Author? Genre? Factors that influence how a person assigns weights and categories

Levels of discourse matter because they help students move from the specific to the general, and to develop metacognitive awareness and flexibility with the subject.

1. Communication Level. The Communication Level focuses on the audience, and involves adjusting the presentation of the message to meet the needs of the intended audience
*Reader can also try to imagine the author and the author's reasons for the arguments

2. Genre Level. The Genre Level "assigns the text to one or more rhetorical categories" (Graesser)
*Text genres can be narrative, expository, persuasive, descriptive
*If a person believes the narrative to be from a newspaper, they will process it differently than if they think it is a from a work of literature.
*Literature tends to be compared with other novels of the same genre; newspaper articles tend to be read in terms of connections with one's experience or other events in the world.

The Comprehension Mechanism:

Three aspects of the comprehension mechanism:
1. Code: Needs to understand the language and the genre
2. Process: Activate relevant knowledge
3. Skill: be able to identify the appropriate meaning-making strategy

The reader's background is important, and as is his or her experience in problem-solving and interpreting text.

*Knowledge of the world influences text comprehension
        Action: Link to outside resources
        Action: Relate to what readers are likely to know

Conclusions, Recommendations, and Implications.

*Background knowledge is useful and helps trigger the transfer of information

*Negative transfer can happen when there are no points of contact and students relate things to the wrong items.

*Superficial similarities between things helps speed the data transfer

*Experts will have a different experience with text than novices. Spontaneous connections will be made, whereas novices will need to have pathways defined for them. It is also helpful to provide novices with background material, such as links.

*People prefer causal structures

*Construction-integration occurs in the analytical process, and creates neural networks, or mind-mapping.

*Embodied cognition (Glenberg, 1997) suggests one should limit the meaning of something to what it means in the real world, and not the potential denotative meanings embodied in the language

*Avoid abstract symbols, concepts represented in a way that acknowledges limitations based on real world / real body.

Useful References

Davidson, J. E., & Sternberg, R. J. (2003) *The psychology of problem-solving.* Cambridge: Cambridge University Press.

Glenberg, A. M. (1997) What memory is for. *Behavior and Brain Sciences,* 20, 1-55.

Glenberg, A.M., Wilkinson, A.A., and Epstein, W. (1982) The Illusion of Knowing: Failure in the Assessment of Comprehension. *Memory & Cognition, 10,* 597-602.

Graesser, A. C., & Clark, L. F. (1985). *Structures and procedures of implicit knowledge.* Norwood, NJ: Ablex.

Graesser, A. C., & Millis, K. K., & Zwaan, R. A. (1997). Discourse comprehension. *Annual Review of Psychology, 48,* 163-189.

Graesser, A. C., McNamara, D., VanLehn, K.. (2005) Scaffolding Deep Comprehension Strategies Through Point&Query, AutoTutor, and iSTART. *Educational Psychologist* **40**:4, 225-234

Graesser, A. C., Singer, M., & Trabasso, T. (1994). Constructing inferences during narrative text comprehension. *Psychological Review, 101,* 371-395.

Hacker, D.J., Dunlosky, J., and Graesser, A.C. Eds.). (1998). *Metacognition in Educational Theory and Practice.* Mahwah, NJ: Erlbaum.

van Dijk TA, Kintsch W. (1983). *Strategies of discourse comprehension.* New York: Academic Press.

Voss JF, Silifies LN. (1996). Learning from history text: the interaction of knowledge and comprehension skill with text structure. *Cognit Instruction;* 14: 45–68.

Rehumanizing the e-Learning Space

Although it might be efficient to set up a fully automated, fully functioning learning space, minded by HAL from *2001, A Space Odyssey*, very few students will actually finish their courses in that charming, fully sanitized and free from human frailty utopia. Why is that? That's a good question.

The problem boils down to boredom, self-doubt, and lack of motivation. The more human the environment, the more likely it is to engage the student's emotions, and make them really CARE about their course.

Further, students become bored, impatient, or even angry when they believe that their time is being wasted, or that their studies are irrelevant. Connecting to a human being often means taking the time to "listen" in the highly visual, often text-centered virtual environment. It also means taking the time to design activities that will maximize the students' points of contact with each other, seek and discover what they have in common.

By doing so, one establishes connection between course content and the outside world -- the world that means something to the students. Ideally, the connections will tie to students' interests, goals, and experience.

Rehumanization is Easy

Rehumanizing the learning space doesn't have to be complicated or "Super-Tech." In the early days of online education, individuals thought that the best way to rehumanize a distance education experience was to try to replicate the appearance of a classroom. Many departments decided to tape their professors as they delivered lectures, and to deliver them over the internet. The other approach was to create PowerPoint presentations that were then synchronized with slides and contained a space for synchronous chat.

These were classic "talking heads" -- mindnumbingly boring to an audience used to Hollywood and video games. Even worse, that solution was terribly expensive and had a shelf life of about 18 months -- until the next generation of hardware or software came along.

What happened? Even when the program administrators could overcome the technical difficulties, they found that the students were, in these settings, passive learners. There was a lack of meaningful interaction.

What is "meaningful interaction" anyway?

Meaningful interaction takes place

a. when communities of practice are developed, where people engage in supportive activities (answering each other's questions, etc.);
b. when on-demand skills acquisition takes place in order to perform a task -- for example, you go out to an archive and download an article that helps you accomplish your homework task;
c. when guidance and positive reinforcement is received by an instructor who has learned to "listen" very well in the virtual environment."Listening" is vital in an online environment because it establishes "real" responsiveness - not the coerciveness or ego-crush of an automated response generated through artificial intelligence.

Encourage Community

Even the most basic information about you can be a huge ice-breaker to your students. If they know something about your research interests, your scholarship, your current focus, and your experience, it helps them feel a sense of confidence, and they will trust your guidance. If you let them know something about you as a person, they can attach a human face to you. The visual of this -- the very idea of your humanity -- mediates the learning space. It adjusts the learning space, and the assumptions and values that the student brings to the learning space are subtly adjusted. You are both approachable and human. This is absolutely vital.

"Listening" in e-learning

Now, granted, if you're listening to a podcast or an audio file, you're truly "listening." But the listening I'm talking about is something else. It is, in a nutshell, the moment in which real communication is reached - when the circuit boards light up because the electricity is flowing.

You can show that you're listening by

    a.   making substantive comments to the student's paper or discussion board comments. Don't just say "very good" - explain what it was that made you think a particular passage was effective;

    b.   respond to questions by answering them in a timely fashion and provide the information needed;

    c.   keeping your comments brief, but meaningful. If you write a page-long comment, the student will stop "listening' and start trying to defend herself.

How do you make sure that the learner is "listening?"

    a.   Set a good tone - start each communication with an affirmation;

    b.   Avoid "humor" - (it can come across as sarcasm);

    c.   Ask questions and connect issues to something in your own life and be willing to reveal something about yourself;

    d.   Avoid inflammatory or judgmental words. Imagine how you would react if you received an e-mail, or saw something posted in the discussion board;

    e.   Keep as neutral as possible in the discussion boards - encourage and react to students, but be careful not to exclude some, or target others.

Perhaps the most effective instructional strategy to employ is to design activities that require the student to relate the course content to their lives. This can be as basic as having students keep journals, or to find examples of what they are studying in current news or world events. The events may be ephemeral and the concepts may be abstract. However, when you connect the two, you establish relevancy and emotional engagement.

Bringing Together Online Instruction and Real Life: Putting Content into the Context

If you can take it one step further and allow the student sufficient flexibility to use the content to solve real-life dilemmas, you demonstrate that you care about the well-being of your student. This is golden. Magic can happen at this point.

Avoid skill-and-drill and rote memorization activities. Also avoid over-reliance on the discussion board - an over-reliance on it as the primary method of instruction can be frustrating for students because the comments that the instructor makes are public. It is awkward, and it often appears that the instructor "plays favorites" -- even when that was not the case. Further, one can unconsciously slip into the trap of unwittingly targeting or humiliating someone.

Remember -- dehumanization does not simply mean giving over to automation and avoiding human contact. It also can mean becoming desensitized to individuality, and losing awareness of the fact that the name / face on the screen is a human being with a complex array of beliefs, circumstances, and socio-cultural influences.

The Role of Relevancy in Online Courses

Introduction

Relevancy is central to online curriculum design and course content selection. This paper provides an overview and understanding of relevancy and can serve as a starting point for developing questions for use in deciding how a course can be relevant to a student\'s career, personal, or academic goals, and for developing guidelines for use in helping the student make connections between course content and the ultimate career, personal, and academic goals he or she may have.

Establishing Relevancy

Students who do not immediately perceive how and why the course content is relevant to their career, academic, or personal lives will become disinterested, bored, even angry. But, what masks itself as a quite justifiable and self-righteous anger ("I paid for this! It's not getting me anywhere!" or "What does this have to do with anything? This is wasting my time!") is, upon deeper analysis, a consequence of the deliberate disorganization of an individual's cognitive processes. When something seems "irrelevant" or "meaningless" it is precisely so because the learner has no way to integrate the activity or the cognitive content into his or her existing mental scheme. The confusion that ensues is unpleasant, particularly to an adult learner, because he or she is likely to attach negative narratives to the experience of being "lost."

The role of the instructor (as facilitator and mentor) must be to be able to contextualize the course content and required activities, and to relate them to already mastered work or tasks. Needless to say, this may require patience. More to the point, it requires the instructor to be able to ask appropriate questions in order to find a way to guide the student to making the connections needed to perform well and to demonstrate mastery of the learning objectives.

These pedagogical approaches are supported by philosophers and cognitive specialists who point to a "connectionist" model of cognition, which suggests that cognitive awareness, and thus meaning, are formed when connections are forged from one region of the brain to another. Symbolic logic has meaning only insofar as there are sets of seemingly unrelated meaning associated with it. In other words, the connectionist model posits that symbols in and of themselves are not enough to explain cognition. There must be other associations, which lead to the ability to posit more complex and real-life applications, such as cause-effect relations, historical sequences, identities, etc. These ideas are used in developing the mathematical models used in artificial intelligence computer programs, as well as in decision trees and probabilities (as applied to human behavior).

Making connections

...to additional material and related readings
The student may understand the material, but the comprehension may be incomplete, or there may be an inability to apply it or demonstrate a working knowledge. If the facilitator can guide the student to additional readings or material (even if it is anecdotal, or in the form of an example from the instructor\'s own experience), the student will have a more comprehensive knowledge.

...to current events
Applying concepts to current events and/or recent discoveries, writings, or activities helps establish the applicability of the course content to the larger, outside world. On a fundamental level, the student is being guided in the practice of "making sense" of the world, and is being presented alternative strategies for ordering, or making meaning out of one's existence.

...to life experiences
If the facilitator is able to help students make connections so that the student can link life experiences to either the course content or the core concepts under discussion, then learning will take place through what B. F. Skinner termed "operant conditioning." In this case, the student will experience a reinforcement of both previously held knowledge (which

includes beliefs and values), and of the knowledge being presented in the course. Once reinforced, the knowledge can be built upon, and the facilitator can help the student in next-level cognitive skills such as differentiation and discrimination. Assessment exercises should replicate operant conditioning so that the taking of practice tests, the writing of essays and journals, and the preparation of final exams or research papers will further reinforce concepts and reasoning skills.

Think About It! Questions for Consideration, Review, or Journal

" When does your course directly address issues that are of immediate interest to your students?
" Name three ways that the content or objectives of your course can make a difference to your students - either in their personal or professional lives, or both.
" Find five websites that can help your students see other perspectives or to make connections between course themes and their lives.
" What are issues that emerge from your course that relate to the world as it is right now, or in the immediate past

Theoretical Underpinnings:

Green, Christopher D. (1998) Are Connectionist Models Theories of Cognition?. http://philsci-archive.pitt.edu/documents/disk0/00/00/02/01/ accessed August 1, 2001

Skinner, B. F. (1976) About Behaviorism. NY: Random House.

Skinner, B. F. and C. B. Ferster (1957) Schedules of Reinforcement. Acton, MA: Copley.

Skinner, B. F. (1953) Science and Human Behavior. NY: Free Press.

Thomas, L. and Harri-Augstein, S. (1985). Self-organised learning. London: Routledge.

Wilson, Elizabeth A. (1998) Neural Geographies. London: Routledge.

Applied to Online Instruction:
http://hagar.up.ac.za/catts/learner/1999/kgarimetsa_rj/eel880/exaprjct/pedagog.htm

http://portfolios.valdosta.edu/tcdowdy/std7.htm

Why Online Collaborations Fail

Ask online students if there was anything they disliked in their last online course, and you're likely to get a resounding "I hated the group work!" Best practices for online courses tend to place a great deal of importance on collaborative learning, either in the form of discussion boards, or in group projects. But while discussion boards work quite well, depending on the skill of the facilitator and the nature of the questions, group projects are often such miserable failures that they taint the learner's perception of the entire course.

What happened? What went wrong? There are usually many factors, but a few are listed below:

Too complicated. The project contains too many steps to reach the final outcome. The complexity makes it difficult to understand and to delegate work, and to set achievable goals.

Solution: Instead of requiring one large group project, ask the group to do four or five small group projects that will require just two or three steps, rather than dozens.

Time conflicts. Required collaborations do not reflect the real time commitments of the participants, nor do they reflect schedules or time zone differences.

Solution: Give the team at least a week to do each project, no matter how small. Ask the individual team members what they are doing to find out and accommodate each other's time constraints.

Friction between team members. Team members disagree, express frustration, or stop communicating altogether. Some team members are deliberately obstructive, or criticize work, endlessly debate small points, or refuse to contribute at all. Instead of working on the project, the energy of the group is spent in conflict resolution. Some may drop out. Others find they become passive when they believe that their input does not matter, and they let the dominant team members do the work.

Solution: Define the roles as well as the tasks. Provide guidelines for team-member roles, and describe actions to be taken by team members.

Tasks are vague, poorly defined. Although the outcome may be defined and described well, the individual tasks are not clearly defined, nor are they delegated in an effective manner. Tasks are repeated needlessly, or done with contradictory results.

Solution: Define and describe the tasks in terms of what needs to be done, how to do it, and how to present the results.

No clearly defined goal or outcome. The overall goal or desired outcome may be imprecisely described or defined. It is important to clearly define the concrete attributes: length, structure, content, purpose, format, complexity.

Solution: Make sure that the outcome and goals are as clearly defined as possible. "SMART" goal-setting is ideal: Specific, Measured, Achievable, Reasonable, Time-based. Of course, there are down sides to having rigidly defined outcomes. They can inhibit extremely creative and driven students, and they can result in conformity and mediocrity.

Resentment because of lack of work parity. Team members become angry because the work load is not evenly distributed. Some team members may be perceived as slackers or freeloaders, who take credit but refuse to pull their weight. The converse can also be true. There may be resentment because one team member will attempt to dominate and not allow individuals to participate in the process. The dominant person may be perceived as a bully, much to his / her surprise. She thought she was simply being efficient, proactive, and "Type A."

Solution: Listen. List the roles and the behaviors expected of the roles.

Competitive rather than collaborative. Group members are caught up in proving that they are "right" and that the others are not. They do not want to modify any of their work in order to have it mesh or blend with the others to produce a coherent whole.

Solution: Separate the tasks and roles so that there is division of labor, rather than overlap.

No sense of community. There is a failure to bond, and hence a failure to thrive. Collaborations with this problem sometimes never get off the ground.

Solution: Ask team members to post photos, details about themselves that they'd like to share, and to start a discussion board or forum in which they discuss current events and items of interest.

Irrelevant activities. Team members may resist doing activities they perceive to be irrelevant to the overall goal or objective they envisioned when joining the group. Even those who go ahead and do the activities may feel resentful.

Solution: Let the team members know how their work ties into the final objective (the project), and how it ties into a larger world as well.

Collaborative papers require "blending" rather than stand-alone components. The collaboration is expected to produce a paper that flows as though it were written by a single person. This can pose a monumental, even insurmountable, challenge because individual voices, writing styles, even format can be completely at odds. Further problems surface when individual team members resent the way that their work has been edited.

Solution: Develop structures that allow individuals to insert their own work in sections clearly identified as pertaining to them. Do not try to blend or mesh the parts.

These are only a few suggestions. There are more, which will be presented at a later date. At that time, there will also be a discussion of types of collaboration projects that work well, and examples will be provided.

career, personal, or academic goals, and for developing guidelines for use in helping the student make connections between course content and the ultimate career, personal, and academic goals he or she may have.

Establishing Relevancy

Students who do not immediately perceive how and why the course content is relevant to their career, academic, or personal lives will become disinterested, bored, even angry. But, what masks itself as a quite justifiable and self-righteous anger ("I paid for this! It's not getting me anywhere!" or "What does this have to do with anything? This is wasting my time!") is, upon deeper analysis, a consequence of the deliberate disorganization of an individual's cognitive processes. When something seems "irrelevant" or "meaningless" it is precisely so because the learner has no way to integrate the activity or the cognitive content into his or her existing mental scheme. The confusion that ensues is unpleasant, particularly to an adult learner, because he or she is likely to attach negative narratives to the experience of being "lost."

The role of the instructor (as facilitator and mentor) must be to be able to contextualize the course content and required activities, and to relate them to already mastered work or tasks. Needless to say, this may require patience. More to the point, it requires the instructor to be able to ask appropriate questions in order to find a way to guide the student to making the connections needed to perform well and to demonstrate mastery of the learning objectives.

These pedagogical approaches are supported by philosophers and cognitive specialists who point to a "connectionist" model of cognition, which suggests that cognitive awareness, and thus meaning, are formed when connections are forged from one region of the brain to another. Symbolic logic has meaning only insofar as there are sets of seemingly unrelated meaning associated with it. In other words, the connectionist model posits that symbols in and of themselves are not enough to explain cognition. There must be other associations, which lead to the ability to posit more complex and real-life applications, such as cause-effect relations, historical sequences, identities, etc. These ideas are used in developing the mathematical models used in artificial intelligence computer programs, as well as in decision trees and probabilities (as applied to human behavior).

Making connections

...to additional material and related readings
The student may understand the material, but the comprehension may be incomplete, or there may be an inability to apply it or demonstrate a working knowledge. If the facilitator can guide the student to additional readings or material (even if it is anecdotal, or in the form of an example from the instructor's own experience), the student will have a more comprehensive knowledge.

...to current events
Applying concepts to current events and/or recent discoveries, writings, or activities helps establish the applicability of the course content to the larger, outside world. On a fundamental level, the student is being guided in the practice of "making sense" of the world, and is being presented alternative strategies for ordering, or making meaning out of one's existence.

...to life experiences
If the facilitator is able to help students make connections so that the student can link life experiences to either the course content or the core concepts under discussion, then learning will take place through what B. F. Skinner termed "operant conditioning." In this case, the student will experience a reinforcement of both previously held knowledge (which includes beliefs and values), and of the knowledge being presented in the course. Once reinforced, the knowledge can be built upon, and the facilitator can help the student in next-level cognitive skills such as differentiation and discrimination. Assessment exercises should replicate operant conditioning so that the taking of practice tests, the writing of essays and journals, and the preparation of final exams or research papers will further reinforce concepts and reasoning skills.

Think About It! Questions for Consideration, Review, or Journal

" When does your course directly address issues that are of immediate interest to your students?
" Name three ways that the content or objectives of your course can make a difference to your students - either in their personal or professional lives, or both.
" Find five websites that can help your students see other perspectives or to make connections between course themes and their lives.
" What are issues that emerge from your course that relate to the world as it is right now, or in the immediate past

Theoretical Underpinnings:

Green, Christopher D. (1998) Are Connectionist Models Theories of Cognition?. http://philsci-archive.pitt.edu/documents/disk0/00/00/02/01/ accessed August 1, 2001
Skinner, B. F. (1976) About Behaviorism. NY: Random House.
Skinner, B. F. and C. B. Ferster (1957) Schedules of Reinforcement. Acton, MA: Copley.
Skinner, B. F. (1953) Science and Human Behavior. NY: Free Press.
Thomas, L. and Harri-Augstein, S. (1985). Self-organised learning. London: Routledge.
Wilson, Elizabeth A. (1998) Neural Geographies. London: Routledge.
Applied to Online Instruction:
http://hagar.up.ac.za/catts/learner/1999/kgarimetsa_rj/e el880/exaprjct/pedagog.htm
http://portfolios.valdosta.edu/tcdowdy/std7.htm

Review of *What Video Games Have to Teach Us About Learning and Literacy*

In *What Video Games Have to Teach Us About Learning and Literacy* (2004), James Paul Gee has written what is perhaps one of the most important books to be published in the last several years on video games, cognition, and e-learning. His book essentially bridges the theory gap that has been widening between the principles of e-learning and video game-based simulations, multi-player role-playing or narrative-based interactive video games.

Gee, a distinguished professor of reading at the University of Wisconsin has written an extremely accessible book that takes a close look not only at specific video games, but also examines how the games are played. The quest for understanding why children learn video games apparently in a vacuum and completely on their own is a paradox in our current culture of formal education. Gee shows how children and adults master the games, revealingly, without the benefit of proscribed classroom exercises, workshops, or formalized online learning modules. What makes Gee's text so valuable is that he goes through a long list of learning principles and demonstrates how each one manifests itself when individuals learn and master video games.

Gee's primary thesis is that our educational system has failed us. The classroom, as it is today, bores and frustrates both students and teachers. It is not a question of funding or resources, but a misguided emphasis on rote memorization, passive "skill and drill," irrelevant curriculum, and material detached from the world, individuals, and society around it. Initiatives such as "No Child Left Behind" are doing nothing at all to correct this; if anything, according to Gee, such programs exacerbate the problem by extending the distance between effective and ineffective instructional strategies.

What makes this book enjoyable is that Gee takes a long list of learning principles and makes them come alive in the mind of the reader by using a child's process of learning a video game as an illustrative example. Gee avoids the usual pitfalls - he neither "dumbs down" the theory nor restricts it to a certain age group. What usually troubles one about books that involve learning theory is that they are often meta-textual and painfully self-reflexive - theory about theory. With Gee, the concepts return to their appropriate provenances: cognitive psychology, neurology, behaviorism, sociology, developmental psychology. In essence, what Gee is doing is providing experimental / experiential grounding in an informal way, and thus supporting the validity of the theories themselves. Thus, the reader can move to the outstanding footnotes and excellent appendix to find the history of the ideas, seminal studies, and key researchers in the various fields. The book is a treasure trove of resources and concepts without ever being clunky or painful.

Gee takes a holistic approach to the analysis of cognitive and behaviorist actions engaged in video games. He confronts something that often confounds educators who design learning materials for pre-schoolers and early elementary levels: How is it that young learners, who are restless, suffer from a wide spectrum of attention and cognitive challenges, and who are assumed incapable of abstract thinking, complex problem-solving, feats of memory, and fine motor skills, are able to sit for hours in rapt, focused attention as they accomplish tasks of remarkable complexity. At their computers, they build buildings, cities, worlds, and engage with multiple opponents, and multi-task in a dynamic environment.

Divided into conceptual blocks, *What Video Games Have to Teach Us* clusters learning theories as applied to video games into the categories corresponding to semiotics, identity construction, situated meaning, narratives, word-action relations, cultural grammars, and social constructivism. One of the aspects that is most appealing about Gee's book is that it is simultaneously an adventure and a storage system. Gee engages one in a journey where it is possible to observe a person learning and exploring popular video games while it constructs a convenient conceptual file cabinet where one can mentally archive and retrieve the 36 learning principles that he considers to be foundational to learning, whether it be in traditional classrooms or in hand-on applications.

Although Gee's book ostensibly addresses early childhood development and K-12 education, the concepts and theories are applicable to adult and non-traditional learners as well. For example, Gee was a presenter at the sold-out, standing-room only Serious Games Summit D.C., held October 18 - 19, 2004, in Washington, D.C. In the two-day affair, video game developers and users of distributed, multi-player interactive training met and discussed trends and new developments. Representatives of the military, higher education, health industry, and urban planners explored ways that games and gaming can transcend entertainment, or move beyond expensive and difficult to change simulations. The idea is to deliver distributed education solutions in ways that result in "deep learning," by employing just the techniques that Gee describes in his book: "just in time learning," scaffolding, relevant tasks, connections to a social group, projected identities, identification, and more.

What Video Games Have to Teach Us About Learning and Literacy Publisher: Palgrave Macmillan (New York), ISBN: 1403965382 (paperback edition) 240 pages, List price: $15.95 (paperback version)

Constructivists 'R' Us: Pick the Epistemology that Works for You

When it comes to learning theories and epistemologies, I think I'm a constructivist. Yes, that's what I am -- and about 99.9 % of all other people involved in online education. But what does being a constructivist actually mean?

Radical constructivism is what psychologist Ernst von Glaserfeld has characterized as a radical "theory of knowledge in which knowledge does not reflect an objective, ontological reality but exclusively an ordering and organization of a world constituted by our experience" (von Glasersfeld, 1984, p.24). What happens when you have limited experience? How does he account for the fact that people may have shared experiences, but they perceived them completely differently? It seems to me that there would be an utter and complete breakdown of communication. Would ANYONE have the same language? Would ALL language be a kind of Wittgensteinian "private language"? That's what it sounds like to me.

Social constructivism is much more palatable for most people. It suggests that reality is an agreed-upon construct, gradually negotiated or mediated by a group. It has been explained by some that social constructivism "sees consensus between different subjects as the ultimate criterion to judge knowledge. 'Truth' or 'reality' will be accorded only to those constructions on which most people of a social group agree" (Heylighen, 1993p.2).

If I back up a minute and take a look at constructivism, I realize that constructivism doesn't always work too well online. However, it certainly seems to at first – after all, the promise held out that meaning can be agreed upon by invoking collective experience, and establishing connections.

Invoking collective shared experience and establishing connections is often easier said than done. The e-learning space is often either too ambiguous or too rigid and overly defined. There can also be too much structure, or a lack of structure.

However, I still maintain that I'm a constructivist. I do think that people make meaning by means of connections, and we learn what is meaningful and what is NOT meaningful by means of social conventions.

I don't think it is possible to take the cognitive out of the constructivist epistemology.

The **cognitive** (and connectionist) ideas of mind and meaning-making help explain why and how reality becomes constructed in the mind of the world.

I also like the notion that behaviorism can be employed. Perhaps I have fantasies of power. I love the idea that sensory - cognitive- behavior triggers exist in combinations of colors, images, sounds, etc. It starts sounding very science fiction -- and, one can't help but think of the various attempts to modify behavior. I enjoy thinking of fictional depictions -- **A Clockwork Orange** comes to mind. Kafka does, too. (!) Of course, an online university is not a penal colony or a reform school -- but I just love the possibilities. It would be nice to make an environment creates a "pleasure dome" effect -- hmmm -- wasn't that what "virtual learning space" was supposed to be about? I remember the hype about being able to put on the "virtual reality glasses" and really get into the space.

I suspect we're getting there when we start incorporating sims and "serious games" in online or hybrid classes. So far, I haven't incorporated any in my classes, except I did make Tom Clancy's "Splinter Cell" an option in one class.

Now, there's more to the story. If I drill down, I think at heart, I'm a **postmodernist** and I love the notions of "meaning in flux" and that the world is a text to be deconstructed. Learning to "read" the world as a text -- to decode the signs and messages in the signs / symbols / codes around us – is powerful stuff. It can even be dangerous in the wrong regime. In some countries you really dare not "read" political campaign posters, slogans, architecture, iconography, and artwork. In Turkmenistan, for example, it might be a bit dangerous to impute meaning to the monuments to the great leader, Turkmenbashi. (See "Monuments in Ashkabat" http://www.galenfrysinger.com/turkmenbashi.htm)

The pitfall with that approach is that students sometimes become upset or offended when their sacred cows get butchered. I remember some rather heated class discussions after looking at the images of femininity contained in Disney films.

I'd really like to dig into Edward Tolman's work on rats and mazes and explore the dark side of operant conditioning. I'm also intrigued by "extreme conditioning." This is probably wrong of me, but there you have it. I wonder if there is a particular icon on a computer screen that is UTTERLY irresistible, and one is incapable of not clicking. If so, I think that amazon.com has found it.

If operant conditioning works so well, does this mean that *The Manchurian Candidate* is true? Does it mean that such things happen every day? That's a frightening possibility.

So – I guess that if I were to choose an epistemology, I'd still go with constructivism -- mainly for the flexibility and the situated outcomes that can be tied to one's real-life needs & interests; b) cognitive -- for the "file cabinets" we can put in our minds for archiving and retrieving information; c) behaviorist -- for reinforcing positive behaviors (and the still unrealized fantasy that some day I will be able to train myself to run on a treadmill / exercise wheel like a hamster and really like it).

Helpful References

Bruner, Jerome. (1990). Acts of Meaning. Cambridge, MA: Harvard University Press.

Hanley, Susan (1994). On Constructivism. http://www.inform.umd.edu/UMS+State/UMD-Projects/MCTP/Essays/Constructivism.txt

Honebein, P. (1996). Seven goals for the design of Constructivist learning environments. In B. Wilson, *Constructivist learning environments*, pp. 17-24. New Jersey: Educational Technology Publications.

Simon. Herbert. (1982). *Models of Bounded Rationality* , 2 volumes.

von Glasersfeld, E. (1984). An introduction to radical constructivism. In P. Watzlawick, *The Invented Reality*, (pp.17-40). New York: W.W. Norton & Company.

von Glasersfeld, E. (1987). Learning as a constructive activity. In C. Janvier, *Problems of representation in the teaching and learning of mathematics*, (pp.3-17). New Jersey: Lawrence Erlbaum Associates, Inc.

von Glasersfeld, E. (1989). Constructivism in education. In T. Husen & N. Postlewaite (Eds.), *International Encyclopedia of Education* [Suppl.], (pp.162-163). Oxford, England: Pergamon Press.

von Glasersfeld, E. (1995). A constructivist approach to teaching. In L. Steffe & J. Gale (Eds.). (1995). *Constructivism in education*, (pp.3-16). New Jersey: Lawrence Erlbaum Associates, Inc.

von Glasersfeld, E. (1995b). Sensory experience, abstraction, and teaching. In L. Steffe & J. Gale (Eds.). *Constructivism in education*, (pp.369-384). New Jersey: Lawrence Erlbaum Associates,Inc.

von Glasersfeld, E. (1996).Introduction: Aspects of constructivism. In C. Fosnot (Ed.), *Constructivism: Theory, perspectives, and practice*, (pp.3-7). New York: Teachers College Press.

Vygotsky, L. (1978). *Mind in Society: The Development of Higher Psychological Processes* MA: Harvard University Press.

Watson, J. B. *(1913)* "Psychology As the Behaviorist Views It" *Psychology Review*

Wilson, B. & Cole, P. (1991) A review of cognitive teaching models. *Educational Technology Research and Development*, 39(4), 47-64.

Wilson, B. (1997). The postmodern paradigm. In C. R. Dills and A. Romiszowski (Eds.), *Instructional development paradigms*. Englewood Cliffs NJ: Educational Technology Publications. Also available at: http://www.cudenver.edu/~bwilson/postmodern.html

Stop! You're Scaring Me! Hyperidentities in E-Learning

Fetishizing one's presence on the screen, selecting attributes and appearance to meet the demands of a virtual space, bringing together wish and wish-fulfilment — these are the underlying emotional energizers in many e-learners. Unfortunately, facilitators and instructional designers seek to put limits on the pursuit of transformative potential, and develop instructional strategies that encourage conformity of thought, action, and intellectual input. Why go to such efforts to stifle creative thought? The answer is simple. It is scary. This is particularly the case when text meets image, and the presence of an individual in the e-learning space is highly personalized, and deliberately crafted to evoke an emotional response.

The fact that young e-learners are accustomed to developing hyper-identities in all their online activities often catches instructors by surprise. What is okay in an IM environment or a blog suddenly looks like a cheap bid for attention — sentimental, extreme, moralizing, violent, pornographic, or simply banal. All the "netiquette" in the world won't change this because "netiquette" does not get at the heart of what is happening.

In Miroslaw Filiciak 's essay, "Hyperidentities," a mechanism by which the user (or e-learner) makes the screen a fetish is described. "We make the screen a fetish; we desire it, not only do we want to watch the screen, but also to â€˜be seen' on it" (Filiciak 99). The reasons for being seen on the screen are simple. It is a reification strategy — a way to create oneself, make oneself something. It is simultaneously a process of becoming and being, which centers around images and text projected and manipulated on a screen: "to be visible means to be real," (Filiciak 100).

The idea of self-reification through art is nothing new; nor is the idea of identification with the moving image found on the television or cinematic screen. Further, we seek to masks or alternative identities when the social situation requires it — most often for survival, seduction, or spirituality. Jung explored the way individuals know and understand archetypes, and how they use them to construct masks or personae. When applied to William James' ground-breaking explanation of how individuals present different versions of themselves based on social situations, the possibility of morphing, protean selves presents itself. It is a thousand times amplified in cyberspace, which has drawn people in from its inception precisely because the possibility of masking or remaking oneself exists.

Attempts are made to replicate the social control found in face-to-face interactions by imposing rules, establishing "netiquette" guides, and monitoring chatrooms. Some behaviors are modified, but the underlying issues are not being addressed. It is much more effective to look at channeling what is going on in order to inspire and allow productive persona production, rather than to cuff everyone to a virtual fencepost in the blazing cybersun and watch them writhe miserably and ineffectively.

Here are productive questions:

—How do you modify the social situation so that individuals build masks and play roles that bring them to a deeper understanding of the subject under consideration?

—How do you open up the social situation to encourage true opening up and sharing, rather than flashy attention-seeking?

—How do you know when a person's role-play is creative self-expression or a cry for help — evidence of potentially dangerous patterns of thinking?

—What is the precise moment when communicating through avatars and masks begins to make a discussion come alive, and the experiential real merges with the constructed real, or fantasy?

—At what times does the openness of an e-learning space which encourages the assumption of personae and masks (customizable avatars, icons, emoticons, worlds, etc.) begin to result in abusive, predatory, or destructive behaviors?

Perhaps the e-learning space does not have the same overall feel as a MMORG (Massively Multiplayer Online Roleplaying Game), but it does engage the same energies and fundamental psychological / sociological energies. The potential is there, particularly for those facilitators and instructional designers who are brave of heart and strong of stomach (!)

References and Useful Resources

Filiciak, Miraslaw. "Hyperidentities" in *The Video Game Theory Reader.* NY: Routledge, 2003: 87-102.

In Hurricanes and Helicopters:
E-Learners In Extremus

Failing the E-Learner *In Extremus*: Where Online Courses Can Miss the Mark

Between hurricanes, tsunamis, earthquakes, and war: crazy lives...

It's easy to take the enlisted or young officer's tuition assistance money. But in so doing, many colleges and universities betray a fundamental trust by providing a substandard online learning experience in exchange for their money or indebtedness. It is not unusual for online courses with deployed military personnel to have completion rates as low as 30 percent. Blaming this on the conditions of the military or on the Secretary of Defense is a way of avoiding responsibility. Instead, universities and colleges must respond by analyzing their programs and processes, and make a good-faith effort to make the necessary changes.

When accepting military contracts and students, universities must keep in mind that in an all-volunteer military, many enlisted in order to pay for college, and they are putting their lives on the line, in harm's way for years on end in order to have access to education, and thus a future for themselves and their families. They may not have the background that some of the more privileged students may have, and will require more support services. Further, they are often under enormous stress -- psychological, physical, and time-related -- and accommodations should be made.

Below are the top reasons for failure in an online course delivered to the military. This is a brief overview. Each topic could be an entire article, and will be dealt with at a later date. In the meantime, it is important to realize that to provide effective e-learning for military involves a commitment of financial, intellectual, and human resources.

Failure to Communicate with Student: This is probably the top reason for failure, and simultaneously the easiest and the most difficult to remedy. The student does not receive emails or announcements which give instructions for course procedures, registration, or financial issues. Multiple attempts to communicate with the student (without spamming) should be made. There should be adequate redundancy in the system.

There should be a clear chain of approach:

a. faculty first-line, personalized communication (email, postings, etc.)
b. department-level communication
c. centralized quality-control entity for needs assessments, calendars with timelines, formative evaluations, summative evaluations, general announcements.

Poorly Defined Learning Outcomes: The deployed student does not always have the luxury of a phone call, and chat rooms are often ineffective due to time zone differences and time of online access. If the deployed student has a total of 20 minutes of connectivity on the "morale computers," it is not easy to work out misunderstandings about what he/she is supposed to learn in a class.

Learning outcomes should be

a. clearly stated in words
b. illustrated through tasks
c. modeled with successful examples.

Badly Designed Instructional Tasks: It is one thing to design an instructional task, and it is another thing altogether to do it. It is easy to forget that even the simplest tasks take much more time and have much higher level of complexity if students are accessing through a slow modem, in an internet café environment, or have frequent interruptions due to conditions in wartime. A specialist should take a look at the way that the learning management system is being used and to try to minimize the number of times one must change from screen to screen (each requiring painfully slow reload times). Tasks requiring long time online (connectivity), (online quizzes and tests), involved research that cannot be downloaded, and course content that cannot be downloaded and saved to a local drive will be doomed to failure. Timed access -- tests, digital drop boxes, and other items that automatically shut down after certain amount of time will block the student, as will tasks that are either timed, or require specific times of access.

Inaccessible or Late Course Materials : If it is not possible to obtain course books or materials in a timely fashion, accommodations should be made so that the students can obtain the content in a different manner, at least for the first few weeks. One effective manner is to phase in the use of the textbooks, and to make the materials available online for the first quarter or third of the class.

Faculty Out of Loop -- Can't Perform Basic Tasks : Faculty members are absolutely central to the success of any online program. They need to have achieved a basic level of competence in skills as well as instructional strategies. Further, they need to have readily available support and mentoring, in order to avoid the sense of isolation that so often occurs. Because course and online instruction procedures vary from college to college, it is important to offer ongoing online support and mentoring to faculty -- *avoid the idea of training as the one-time "inoculation."*

Too Many Intermediaries in Support Services : When there are administrative intermediaries in the instructional loop, unexpected snags can happen as students communicate to the intermediary for answers to questions, when the question should have been directed to the faculty member. Intermediaries need to understand the nature of process and be able to identify when to "escalate" the question to the education partner, and avoid wasting time "circling" or "ping-ponging" in fruitless back-and-forths that do not address the real issues.

Courses Not Aligned with Needs of Students: Courses and course curricula lose their freshness and should be updated each time offered. A complete course and curriculum review / retuning should be done each two or three years, depending on the topic and the rate of change. Knowledge management is very important, and a team of subject matter experts should review (rather than just one subject matter expert.) Relevancy and timeliness are keys to deep learning and engagement. Without it, there are few or no incentives. Decisions should not be made "on high" and far removed, but be made with as much connection to real students and faculty as possible.

Failure to Provide Writing Support: Mentoring in academic writing should be provided. The students should be guided and be provided support in everything from composition, grammar, syntax, organization, persuasion, and argumentation to academic research, citation, library resources. Instead of making it a separate activity, it should flow with the actual needs of courses, and be provided in ways that naturally integrate with achieving the learning outcomes for each learning unit, and course. It should also apply to the overall program.

Inappropriate Assessment Strategies: Testing and assessment should be natural outgrowths of the learning activities in the course. Learning activities should involve practice (conceptual, cognitive, and even skill-driven) practice for the actual assessment. Assessment strategies and tips should be included as well.

Learning Management System Issues: How difficult is it to utilize is the learning management system? Is there an over-reliance on it? How granular and re-usable are the learning objects, or the "building blocks" that are being used to populate the learning management system? What is the scalability of the model?

An online tutorial for using the online learning system is rarely enough. Instead, the learning tasks should be made in such a way that the student can master the learning management system through self-exploration.

Key to success: Slowly build in complexity, and add tasks for the student to do. Do not ask the student to master all aspects of the learning management system in Unit One. Build slowly, in an "add-on" manner.

Outdated or Irrelevant Content / Badly Situated Learning:
Learning programs fail to engage soldiers when the material
seems irrelevant, or, even worse -- insulting. Situating learning
means making connection to real-life contexts and tasks, which
emulates apprenticeship. *Know your student and his/her values.
Do not insult them.*

**Rigid Deadlines and Policies, Counterproductive
Administrative Policies:** In seeking efficiency, colleges and
universities unwittingly set up their deployed military students
for failure, particularly in rigid add-drop dates, Incomplete
policies, and automatic "Failure" grades. They set off a domino
reaction as military policies with tuition assistance, etc. are
activated. *Policy should be set so that it coordinates with
military policies, and should not further complicate things.*

No Redundancy in Case of Component Breakdown: What
happens when a unit or component in the course breaks down,
due either to connectivity issues or scheduling? The key is to
have a back-up and to build in redundancy. For example, if a
student cannot post to the discussion board because the
computer has extreme security and firewalls, the student should
have an alternative way to complete course requirements.

Hard-to-Access Library Resources: Libraries are working to
reduce the size of scanned documents and researching new ways
to zip files so that they do not take so much time. Further,
multimedia delivery must be made more efficient -- utilizing
some of the techniques of XBox Live and massively multiplayer
role-playing games. In the meantime, it is important not to lock
content up behind layer upon layer of password protection.

War and Post-War Stress Issues: Finally, courses should be
designed to be as streamlined, useful, and engaging as possible.
They should connect directly with the academic, career, and
personal goals of the learners. More than anything, they should
respect the fact that many of the military students may be
suffering -- not only the pain and anxiety of separation from
loved ones, and being in harm's way -- but also physically and
psychologically. Recent studies have suggested that one in 11
soldiers will suffer from post-traumatic stress syndrome. In

addition to psychological issues, according to many sources, more than 12,000 soldiers in the recent war on terror have suffered from serious and disabling injuries. These soldiers deserve respect and are entitled to accommodation. We must not betray their trust.

Network-centric Warfare and Implications for Distributed Education

The concept of "network centric warfare" has totally pervaded military training and policy publications, and, although there are operational and philosophical critiques of the concept, the fact remains that it continues to influence the way that the military thinks of itself and its activities.

It represents a profound epistemological change -- not only in terms of how strategy is conceptualized, but the entire notion of what constitutes meaning and knowledge. In a certain way, the notion of network-centric warfare privileges knowledge and knowledge management, suggesting that victory has to do with successful management and dissemination of data.

We've seen spectacular successes. Desert Storm is often cited as an excellent example of coordinated information and joint force efforts resulting in overwhelming force, and a quick, harsh, decisive victory. The rise of remote sensing (which evolved quantum leaps from where it was in the late 1970s with LANDSAT satellite imagery, and the ability to generate false color composites and map vegetation, landmasses, and human activity trends in new ways) coupled with highly mobile, handheld GPS units not only transformed land navigation, it also led to breathtaking detail (if not precision) of surface features and heat signatures. Tracking people, natural phenomena, static and mobile features (buildings, equipment, etc.) while coordinating logistics, materials and "fire" could lead the impression that the war of the future (or of today) would be something from a science fiction film. Certainly the footage that the average civilian like myself would see reinforced that notion. "Surgical strikes" of insurgent hideouts in Kosovo, with scary fire coming from gunships, and remotely directed attacks on distant targets, ranging from Sarajevo to wherever, made warfare seem like a techies' game.

According to John Gilligan, the U.S. Air Force's Chief Information Officer, the accuracy and precision of air strikes have become even more astonishing. In a Air Force press release, Gilligan was cited as saying the following: " In Desert Shield/Desert Storm, 40 percent of the munitions that we delivered were precision munitions. Today it's over 90 percent. Our accuracy rate is phenomenal. And when you talk to those who are doing the planning of weapons delivery, we're able to gain insight in terms of what's the physical composition of the target. What are the wind speeds? What's the angle, et cetera? They can predict with extraordinary accuracy what is going to be the collateral damage. Now that's not just what's the impact point, it's what's the collateral damage. All of that is information-based. All of that information is available through the network" (US Fed News, 28 March 2005).

And then comes Fallujah. An then Najaf, Sadr City , and all the other places where the other ubiquitous term, "asymmetric warfare," comes in to play.

Needless to say, in this case, network centric warfare, according to the people who are typically on the ground -- Marines, Infantry, and now, Army National Guard -- has come under fire.

In the April 2005 issue of the *Proceedings* of the U.S. Naval Institute, Captain Tim Feist of the U. S. Marine Corps takes issue with the inflated expectations and hints of invincibility that the "network centric warfare" model suggests. In "Transformation Has Limits," he points out the failures of networks and information, and argues that the raw material and data are often faulty, as are the networks themselves, and the assumptions used to build the models. There is also a suggestion that an over-reliance on it can lead to strategic disasters. This not only has to do with what we are commonly led to think of as "insurgents" -- snipers, suicide bombers, child soldiers, and the trickery of booby-traps and human shields.

What is often not mentioned are the virtual economic blockades that arise due to illicit profiteering -- mercenaries, arms-trafficking, black-marketing, etc. How many ambushed convoys and supply lines are actually types of piracy? How many kidnappings of truck drivers were not expressions of holy war, but of a turf battle over which contractor would receive the lion's share of contracts? How many of the contractor killings were attempts to drive out the lower-paid workers who came in from Nepal , Kenya , Pakistan , and Bangladesh ?

Corruption -- whether originating due to a local "kleptocrat" leader, or de facto "pirates" who take advantage of anarchy and chaos to peddle guns, water, and false documents, along with trafficking humans to provide "safe" passage to somewhere else -- can defeat a network centric war plan, as well as "boots on the ground." Asymmetric warfare is not just about small, unexpected guns against the big ones, it's also about duplicity, double-dealing, and greed.

The astute observer can see a very clear parallel between this situation and that of distributed education. While the disruptive technology has already happened -- the reliance on networks and network information to make decisions and coordinate action (of all types) -- the fact remains that the technology can be rendered useless by ground activities when and if the goal is to control activities in urban centers on the ground.

Network centric warfare can also be rendered useless by incompetence or hubris in the data gathering process. The old "garbage in -- garbage out" tenet still holds.

What does this have to do with military training and education? In a network-centric approach, the following elements hold true:

Training / educational content is distributed over networks: "Coordinated autonomy" is possible through a central network. Entire learning network systems can be in place, with collaboration, contribution, and decentralized access and contribution to a network-housed structure, where the content is housed.

Simulation and video-game based training will take place far from the actual place of battle: Learning will take place far from where the instructor is, and the participants may be separated in time and in space. Yet, they will be united through a massively multiplayer system that allows interaction and coordination. Knowledge gained will be useful, or useless --

depending on its relevancy and "freshness." In such cases, being "stale" but not knowing it will result in a very perniciously deleterious product. In a word, it can kill.

Data used to develop training and "situated" learning will come from far away: The inputs used to create learning modules, learning objects, and the integrated systems will be contributed to the network from widely divergent sources. Coordination is key. Security must constantly be examined. Security will probably always be one step behind the hackers. Even now, researchers are exploring how to probe enemy communication webs in wartime. The same applies to e-learning.

Training created by people who have second-hand or third-hand knowledge can be flawed: Extreme situatedness is a must. Data to build learning programs that is collected on site and uplinked through handhelds in situations as directly related to the real thing as possible is critical. This used to be called "ground truthing." Today is falls into the category of collaborative, multi-nodal course / training development. Training must be reviewed and updated continuously, as circumstances and conditions (as well as tactics) continuously change.

Corruption can destroy the integrity of a learning system. Corruption takes many forms in terms of training and education. Academic dishonesty, theft of intellectual property, and "short-cutting" to simply pander to perceived business opportunities rather than providing a high-quality product are all issues to be addressed. Duplicity, disinformation, political backstabbing, and black-marketeering may not play the same role in an education system as they do in a war-torn country. Nevertheless, one has to say that the sterile view from above (in the control rooms of the networks) has little or no connection with the ugly streets of war where wild dogs fight over human carcasses. Does the analogy hold in higher education or in corporate training? You, the reader, can decide.

To backtrack a bit and to provide grounding for readers who may not be aware of the nuances of network centric warfare, the following is offered.

At a recent briefing and update, David Alberts, director of research and strategic planning in the Office of the Assistant Secretary of Defense for Networks and Information Integration, provided a broad, theoretical overview of network centric warfare. The architect of what was often referred to as information technology warfare, Alberts has influenced policymakers in the Pentagon for a number of years. Here are his words, from the press release:

Network centric warfare has four simple tenets. It all starts with the concept of a robustly networked force. That robustly networked force leads to increased information sharing.

Second, increased information sharing enhances not only the quality of information but encourages collaboration and increases what we call shared awareness.

Third, increased collaboration and shared awareness enables self-synchronization.

Fourth, all of that together dramatically improves mission effectiveness and ability.

These four tenets serve to define a value chain that links the full spectrum of material and non-material investments to operational effectiveness and agility.

*Although these tenets are very general and have broad applicability, there were many people who thought that it was only about the conduct of high intensity **warfare**. So to better convey the notion that these principles are general, we started using the term **network centric** operations sometimes instead of and sometimes with **network centric warfare.*** (US Fed News, 28 March 2005)

The controversy is only beginning. Certainly it will continue to gain momentum as casualties mount, and call into the question the efficacy of a plan that assumes that remotely directed fire and remotely gathered information can truly result in total control of the ground environment.

The argument in education is only beginning, too. Can we assume that remotely delivered educational experiences that take place completely in a digital environment can truly result in total control of the learning outcome?

Appropriate Technology Applied to Online and Distance Education

Appropriate technology considerations are driving many education decisions with respect to the content delivery methods, infrastructure, hosting, and hardware selection. In addition to cutting costs, organizations of all types are looking closely at how to best deliver online and distance training and education to learners in widely diverse conditions, including remote, often-changing locations with variable levels of access. Infrastructure, hosting, and hardware selection have been stretched to the limit given the rapid evolution of technologies, that, in many cases have been disruptive.

Coined by the economist E.F. Schumacher in his seminal text, *Small Is Beautiful,* the term "appropriate technology" refers to the need to align technology options with the real infrastructure, user abilities, and desired outcomes of a place or situation.

When people usually use the term, appropriate technology, they are referring to "down-teching," which is to say that they are using a low-tech solution instead of a higher-tech one because of the availability of spare parts, power, etc. However, the term can also be used to indicate "up-teching" or "technology piggy-backing" so that the latest, and ostensibly highest-tech solution (often an eclectic or synthesis of solutions) is really the best alternative in a seemingly low-tech environment.

In addition to diverse condition, the military are now facing extreme diversity in terms of content delivery options, both in terms of hardware and software. In the mix now are an array of learner-side options: laptops, handheld computers (Dell Axim, etc.), mp3 players (iPod, etc.) PDAs (Blackberry, Palm, Treo, etc.), highly interactive cell phones (T-Mobile Sidekick), video and DVD players. Ways of getting the content to the learner and providing for collaborative learning are also multiple: access through a portal and a learning management system (Blackboard, WebCT, Desire2Learn, WebTycho, open source-Sakai, etc.), open source content, video-game based simulations and "serious games," Internet telephony (Skype, etc.), weblogs / RSS-driven feeds, audio-blogging CD-ROM, as well as basic print-based learning.

Appropriate Granularity of Learning Objects

Needless to say, the array of possibilities and situations requires one to re-examine many of the issues inherent in online/distance course development and delivery. Problems of content management include the danger of instant obsolescence or short shelf life of material that costs a great deal to develop. Many online learning experts have pointed to learning object repository projects (MERLOT, CAREO) as a solution, at least in terms of sources of truly interchangeable, appropriately granular, re-usable, repurposable objects.

In the meantime, course developers need to keep in mind that objects must now be usable across delivery methods, which include PDA, CD-ROM, and online. Screen sizes will vary and the number of plug-ins and players at one's disposal will vary.

Analyze each course and develop a sense of appropriate format. Develop a general template that accommodates the range of options from PDA to CD-ROM to iPod to laptop.

Objects should be in html, jpeg, mp3, gif, mpeg, and sometimes pdf.

Plug-ins and players should be uniform. Adobe Acrobat, Windows Media Player, are safe bets. Use Flash, Java, and Javascript with discretion.

Make sure that the objects are readable in tiny screens (PDAs) as well as large screens. Provide audio backup and scripts for vision-impaired, and be sure that the colors used are also low-vision friendly. Make sure that text can be read by screen readers such as JAWS.

Avoid items that would precipitate a startle reflex or create distractions. Be aware of design considerations for the cognitively impaired (attention deficit syndrome, etc.)

Incorporate commercially available products when it truly contributes to one's learning outcomes. This includes movies, audio, games, and simulations, as well as assessment tools.

If using web-based assessment interfaces such as Survey Suite or Zoomerang, be sure that they are accessible by the students in a time-frame that is significant.

Alleviating Bandwidth Problems

Security issues with respect to online access make it difficult to implement some of the solutions to alleviating bandwidth bottlenecks which are suggested here. The best approach to obtaining more bandwidth is not necessarily one of laying more fiber-optic cable, getting server farms, and putting in a satellite array, although those of us who love the idea of being in the middle of the biggest and "baddest" supercomputer center on the planet are utterly entranced by that option.

More realistically, the following options will help address bandwidth and access issues.

Have a static html alternative wherever and whenever possible: One of the quickest ways to increase bandwidth usage is to put in a website or application that includes a great deal of dynamic html. For example, universities that implemented "smart" student portals that automatically "remember" student information, as well as customizable information provided "on the fly" (such as local weather conditions, stock market ticker tapes, headline news, recommended consumer product purchases), were often shocked by the numerous crashes and the incredibly slow performance upon launch. The first impulse was to blame students downloading from peer networks (Kazaa, Napster, etc.), but the real culprit was the portal application.

Although it is nice to have the dynamic html application, be sure to provide a static html alternative.

Use Internet security and firewalls that block spyware and Trojans: Even if it is not stealing passwords or your identity, spyware is bad. It sends commands and thus impedes functionality. In effect, too much spyware is a kind of de facto "denial of service" attack, which results in too much information being sent in a very limited space.

Some institutions that eradicated spyware from their servers found their performance improved as much as 75 percent.

Prohibit P2P file sharing: Individuals who allow their computers to be used as mini-servers for interactive games, file sharing (mp3s and mpegs), and games, put a huge stress on a university's or military education unit's computer system. It is going to be difficult to modify all behaviors, and young, bored enlisted troops with high-speed access are going to be the first to download games, music, and videos. Further, with the ever-increasing popularity of interactive games (Xbox Live), it is important to insist that individuals pay for their own access (in-room service, Internet cafe, etc.) rather than clogging military or university networks.

Avoid massive pdf files: It is amazing that someone has not stopped digital resources providers such as EBSCO and Proquest, from scanning in journal articles in such a way as to result in gargantuan file sizes. There is nothing more disappointing that downloading and storing a 3 MB file that is a mere 2 pages when printed. Not only does it make storage an issue, it requires a lot of bandwidth for downloading, and users may find that their connection times out before the download completes. Try to keep scanned files at less than 350 kb.

Separate the course content from the interactive parts of the course (discussion board, chat, gradebook): The interactive elements can often have access issues, due to being blocked by military servers, or being bound up in a learning management system. Having multiple users signed in at the same time can create an overload, as well. Thus, be sure to house audio, text, and graphics content separately.

Utilize alternative means for encouraging student interaction:
Commercial services such as internet telephony (Skype) and the various instant messengers (AIM, MSN, Yahoo), are very efficient and affordable. Collaborative chats can be hosted by free services such as Chatzy.

Use different server for assessment, not requiring access through portal: Bandwidth pressure can also be alleviated by housing tests and assessments on a different server.

Use prepackaged non-interactive components whenever possible: Content and activities can be downloaded onto a chip (in the case of PDAs), onto a CD-ROM, or a card (in the case of games). It is important to maintain good battery life, though, if results are being stored in flash memory rather than on the chip or elsewhere in memory.

Avoid e-mail web access that requires complex applications and a great deal of dynamic html: Outlook and Lotus webmail functions are useful and are often required by universities. They are rendered useless, however, when students cannot access them due to the complex nature of the code, which can include java, flash, dynamic html, java script, etc. The simpler the interface the better. Functionality is useless without access.

Appropriate Interactivity

Some of the policies and procedures that make sense for students who are doing coursework in homes, dorms, offices, or hotel rooms with high-speed internet access do not work for deployed military students, who stand in line for an hour for 15 minutes on the "morale" computer, or spend all their liberty scouring the port for Internet cafes, just to find that access the learning management system has been blocked.

Designers need to rethink the nature of interactivity, and to open it up so that there are easier and more dynamic options. Although one of the major selling points of a learning management system is that it is self-contained, which allows for the easy functioning of interactive databases and a "one stop shopping" learning experience. Further, the fact that a record can be maintained of all correspondence is useful in cases of grade appeals and legal action.

However, is such tight control really necessary? Learning is fluid and arises spontaneously through interaction--with the text, with other students, with the outside world in situated, or experience-based learning.

It is often not a bad idea to experiment with alternative forms of chat and discussion--using other groups, or software (chatzy, yahoo groups).

E-mail forms the core of interactivity between instructor and student, and an increasing number of institutions are requiring students to use the institution's e-mail. This solves certain problems, including the problem of forward e-mail getting trapped in spamguards, and a lack of records about correspondence.

However, if the host institution insists upon its own e-mail, it must make sure that its email server is robust enough to handle the volume, and that it has a low-bandwidth alternative for slow dial-up connections. Further, limits to e-mail size storage restrictions should be lifted. It is pretty ridiculous to require an instructor to use the host institution's email server for all correspondence and to keep a record of student projects and submissions, and then to announce a limit, such as 20 Mb of storage.

Blogs: Not to be Ignored or Avoided Any More

Back in 2000, when blogs were first taking off, they were touted as great places to keep journals and to aggregate one's one news and current events. Journals tended to be confessional and of the "my daily diary" mode, an exercise in confessional literature or narcissism.

However, the notion of how to use blogs has profoundly changed over the last few years. Some of the key events in the "blog-explosion" come to mind as being tied to global world events. While people use to post in alt.net when they had something to say about a current event, rss made blogging the pundit's platform of choice. Pundit-powered blogging took hold with the 2000 election debate, Chandra Levy (and all the conspiracy theories), 9-11, Matt Drudge and others, anthrax, Iraq war, 2004 U.S. presidential election, and more.

There are now hybrid "daily diary" types of blogs--blogs from the front or deployment, even better than e-mail or snail mail, in the sense that one can post photos and daily events without having to send individual e-mails. Blogs use templates that are remarkably flexible and easy to use, and syndication is a snap if one uses programs such as bloglines (http://www.bloglines.com) and feedburner (http://www.feedburner.com)

The more popular weblog providers are blogger (http://www.blogger.com), xanga (http://www.xanga.com), typepad, lycos/tripod, and others.

There are many advantage of using blogs in online education, particularly when access is not a problem. Students can subscribe to the feed, which comes to them through their feed reader of choice. They can aggregate feeds in one of the many free aggregators available: newsgator, bloglines, feedburner. They can also aggregate audio feeds in what is known as podcasts (after the mp3 player, iPod).

Student can comment on blogs, and then develop their own. A companion website can also be developed for free at myspace.com (http://www.myspace.com).

Although there are definite problems with control of content and hosting if one encourages students to develop their own websites and weblogs, as well as audioblogs, the advantages are that the weblogs do not go away at the end of the semester, as do university-provided personal websites and space. Plus, the pressure on the university system is reduced.

Although personal expression and news-based weblogs still predominate, an increasing number of blogs deal with other topics that include science and medicine, music, entertainment, education, journalism, social sciences, health, financial planning, and more. The same applied to audio blogs. Classification and ratings of blogs is provided in ipodder, google alerts, blogstreet, bloglines, and numerous others.

The advangate of blogs is that content is downloadable and playable later. This is particularly useful in the case of PDAs, handhelds, and mp3 players, and could be very appropriate for educational programs used by the Coast Guard and others, where handheld delivery is required.

Graphics

PDA and handheld delivery requires a reassessment of how graphics and learning objects are used, particularly if the graphics are large or interactive.

Most common graphics and interactive graphic applications include the following:
--photos
--illustrations
--diagrams
--maps

It is important to remember that the mouse-overs and other javascript applications will not work in some environments, nor will they work with all browsers (Firefox is one).

Key considerations in developing graphics for appropriate and multiple deployability are

--size
--viewability on different size screens
--color / display issues--will the graphics be readable in grayscale?
--is there sufficient color contrast for vision-impaired learners or in a case of poor color display?

Audio and the Surge in Popularity of mp3 Players

Before the recent price cut in iPods, and the advent of RSS2 which allowed blogs to deliver mp3 content seamlessly as a single download, mp3 files generally consisted of popular music converted to an mp3 and illicitly shared through peer-to-peer (P2P) networks, including Napster, Kazaa, Morpheus, etc.

Now, however, more audio files are being made available, particularly those that average 10 minutes in length and consist of "podcasts" or shows. These are often extemporaneous thoughts, but the best and most useful ones have a text script or outline which appears on the blog website in html.

Such a format is ideal for the deployed military student who may download the file, or receive it on a chip. Having the content in multiple locations--housed on the blog, and also in chip format on a handheld or in an iPod makes listening to lectures possible, even while on a submarine, in a long flight on a transport plane, lying in a tight bunk on a Coast Guard cutter, or during downtime on a large aircraft carrier.

In addition to providing a portable solution to content, the audio files accommodate learning styles, and help the learner who may be more comfortable with audio / aural transmission of ideas.

Further, audio has a direct impact on learner affect, which can be very helpful in alleviating learner anxiety. Audio presentation of information at a time that is comfortable for the learner, when he or she is most receptive is very useful in developing effective self-regulation, which is vital in any learning strategy.

The topic of appropriate technology is certainly a vast one, and considers revisiting, particularly when what is called for is a kind of technology piggybacking as described in the various examples. Solutions are not confined to instructional design, content delivery, or hardware. Large structural issues must be addressed in order to solve such issues as bandwidth, and basic philosophical issues about control and intellectual property must be addressed as well.

Guiding E-Learners: Strategies for Effective Teaching

Instructors need to "rehumanize" themselves when guiding their military personnel students, especially those in "low-contact" asynchronous online courses, as the students are deployed, in combat zones, etc.

1. Too much automation results in a dehumanized learning space

Although it might be efficient to set up a fully automated, fully functioning learning space, minded by HAL from 2001, A Space Odyssey, very few students will actually finish their courses in that charming, fully sanitized and free from human frailty utopia. Why is that? That's a good question. The problem boils down to boredom, self-doubt, and lack of motivation. The more human the environment, the more likely it is to engage the student's emotions, and make them really CARE about their course. Further, students become bored, impatient, or even angry when they believe that their time is being wasted, or that their studies are irrelevant.

2. "Listening" to students in a text-based environment

Connecting to a human being often means taking the time to "listen" in the highly visual, often text-centered virtual environment. It also means taking the time to design activities that will maximize the students' points of contact with each other, seek and discover what they have in common. By doing so, one establishes connection between course content and the outside world -- the world that means something to the students. Ideally, the connections will tie to students' interests, goals, and experience.

3. Avoiding the complicated or "Super-Tech" solutions

In the early days of online education, individuals thought that the best way to rehumanize a distance education experience was to try to replicate the appearance of a classroom. Many departments decided to tape their professors as they delivered lectures, and to deliver them over the internet. The other approach was to create PowerPoint presentations that were then synchronized with slides and contained a space for synchronous chat. These were classic "talking heads" -- mind-numbingly boring to an audience used to Hollywood and video games. Even worse, that solution was terribly expensive and had a shelf life of about 18 months -- until the next generation of hardware or software came along. What happened? Even when the program administrators could overcome the technical difficulties, they found that the students were, in these settings, passive learners. There was a lack of meaningful interaction.

4. Meaningful interaction

Meaningful interaction takes place a) when communities of practice are developed, and people engage in supportive activities (answering each other's questions, etc.); b) when on-demand skills acquisition takes place in order to perform a task -- for example, you go out to an archive and download an article that helps you accomplish your homework task; c) when guidance and positive reinforcement are received by an instructor who has learned to "listen" very well in the virtual environment.

5. "Listening" in an online environment

Listening is important because it establishes "real" responsiveness -- not the coerciveness or ego-crush of an automated response generated through artificial intelligence. Now, granted, if you're listening to me speak in an audio file, you're truly "listening." But the listening I'm talking about is something else. It is, in a nutshell, the moment in which real communication is reached -- when the circuit boards light up because the electricity is flowing.

You can show that you're listening by

a. making substantive comments to the student's paper. Don't simply assign a grade or write "very good." Explain what it was that made you think a particular passage was effective;
b. respond to questions by answering them in a timely fashion and provide the information needed;
c. keep your comments brief, but meaningful.

If you write a page-long comment, the student will stop "listening' and start trying to defend himself or herself. How do you make sure that the learner is "listening?"

a. Set a good tone -- start each communication with an affirmation
b. Avoid "humor" -- (it can come across as sarcasm)
c. Ask questions and connect issues to something in your own life; be willing to reveal something about yourself.
d. Avoid inflammatory or judgmental words. Imagine how you would react if you received an e-mail, or saw something posted in the discussion board.
e. Keep as neutral as possible in the discussion boards -- encourage and react to students, but be careful not to exclude some, or target others.
f. Facilitator self-disclosure can build enthusiasm and encourage intellectual curiosity

Even the most basic information about you can be a huge ice-breaker to your students. If they know something about your research interests, your scholarship, your current focus, and your experience, it helps them feel a sense of confidence, and they will trust your guidance. If you let them know something about you as a person, they can attach a human face to you. The visual of this -- the very idea of your humanity -- mediates the learning space. It adjusts the learning space, and the assumptions and values that the student brings to the learning space are subtly adjusted. You are suddenly imbued with "reasonableness" and compassion. This is absolutely vital.

This is even more important in the case of deployed military students, who are bridging cultures. Needless to say, whether they are on a ship, in an air force base somewhere, or

7. Integrating instructional activities with real-life details; including context in the content

Avoid skill-and-drill and rote memorization activities. Also avoid over-reliance on the discussion board -- a heavy reliance on it, ironically, turns into a dehumanizing experience because individuals with dial-up modems or brief time online find they are wading through too many comments.

Perhaps the most effective instructional strategy to employ is to design activities that require the student to relate the course content to their lives. This can be as basic as having students keep journals, or to find examples of what they are studying in current news or world events. The events may be ephemeral and the concepts may be abstract. However, when you connect the two, you establish relevancy and emotional engagement. If you can take it one step further and allow the student sufficient flexibility to use the content to solve real-life dilemmas, you demonstrate that you care about the well-being of your student. This is golden. Magic can happen at this point.

8. Building trust and confidence through activities that involve revisions or staged, evolutionary tasks

If you were to envision an entire semester spent in various stages of revision, you'd probably curl up in a little ball and hide under your desk or someplace far, far away from your computer and high-speed internet connection. Surprisingly, though, in the online environment, revision activities can be turned (quite productively, in fact) into a form of "listening." Wow! How does this magic occur? you might ask. There are two or three aspects of this that are critical:

a. give your students a chance to write about something they are intrinsically interested in;
b. give them a flow chart or a model to follow for a first draft. This will help them overcome "block," even if they are not too invested in the ideas that come out of that first pass;
c. at the same time, ask them to conduct a literature search (5 to 10 sources), on the topic, and to write a

one-paragraph description. They can learn how to do proper citation, as they are able to discover useful things about a topic that interests them. This is a painless way to learn how to do annotated bibliographies.

d.   ask them to revise their paper, and add the findings from the literature search. Then, respond with guidance and affirmation.

e.   go through two or three more revisions, which will include peer reviews and structural overhauls. Culminate in an "extreme revision" which asks the writer to bulk up the paper in significant ways. The key is that after every revision, respond with substantive, meaningful comments.

What has gone on is, in essence, an accretionary process. I like to think of it as a pearl -- building itself, slowly, layer by beautiful layer. Each step of the way requires creative problem-solving, analytical thinking, synthesis, and invention.

More importantly, you have been a supportive mentor who has listened, and has responded in constructive ways. Your students will appreciate it.

The Instructor and the Online Military Student: A Confession

I've been teaching classes for active-duty military for several years now, and over that time, my thinking has taken huge turns and I've had to confront the fact that my comfort zone ways of thinking are inadequate.

My son is in the desert right now. He's a 20-year-old Lance Corporal of the U.S. Marine Corps and he arrived at 29 Palms, California, last week, to do a 5-week training (which used to be 8-week, but now shortened) to prepare him and others for deployment. I'm a nervous wreck.

In the meantime, I have yet another new perspective on life, and not one that I ever expected to have.

What do you do when you find out that your theories and approaches to life turn out to be a kind of dogma? Sure, it gains you admittance to a small, exclusive coterie of like-minded dogmatic thinkers, but on some level, you've cut yourself off.

When I was in graduate school, many of my favorite theories and critical approaches were, to put it mildly, cryptic. In order to be taken seriously, or even to be listened to at all, one had to demonstrate one's fluency in the specialized language of one's chosen sub-group or sub-discipline. There was something very heady and exhilarating about mastering the discourse - we could speak in the code of the initiates. The fact that no one else could understand us reinforced our sense of being special. We invented our own secret society - not Skull and Bones - but an approximation of that, at least in the sense of self-imbued instant elitism.

How did that prepare me to respond to students?

I have to say that it did not at all. Despite all the emphasis on inclusion, diversity, and the phenomenology of oppression, I was not prepared by the academy to be able to listen to or appreciate another person's vocabulary. I was not prepared in any meaningful way to relate to students. This is not the fault of the courses I had in teaching. Those were actually very good. I'm talking about what existed outside my university - "The Academy" - an elitist, formless, faceless, normative body that exacted absolute conformity of anyone who dared aspire to its ranks. All the while, it denied it required absolute obeisance, a bended knee to the idea that anyone who might question us was, in a word, ignorant.

How did that attitude prepare me to approach online students?

It didn't. What it did was to delude me into thinking that I was open-minded, and that an appropriate instructional goal or learning outcome was to bring students around to my way of thinking.

Somewhere along the line, I had to let go of some of the rigid notions I had. I had to think again.

- What constitutes critical thinking?
- When am I unconsciously pressuring individuals to simply spout dogma or an ideology?
- When is a student simply rephrasing and regurgitating some of the reading, and how can I make myself aware enough to tell?
- And, how to I come to accept that to require students to do that is toxic and potentially demeaning?

I need to find a good mirror.

I need to find a way to be aware of my own biases and prejudices - the most damaging of which are utterly invisible to me. The irony is that the moment I think I've made myself bias-free by immersing myself in the latest critical approach, in reality I've just blinded myself.

It's scary.

When was the moment when I first became aware that I was a creature bred of ill-intentioned programming? When did I realize that I was built to be the way I am? The pathetic lie is that I think I'm open-minded, able to see all sides of an argument, that I'm fair, insightful, patient, and nurturing. The truth is, that's what I'm conditioned to think I am. If something happens to challenge me in my little bubble world, I blame them. "Ah, poor fools. They ARE ignorant, aren't they? They'll turn around after a few years, though…"

I may be exaggerating. I'm not sure, though.

Read Isaac Asimov's *I, Robot*. It can be seen as an extended metaphor of what happens to graduate students. Granted, he didn't intend it as such. But it is there, all the same.

For years, I thought of myself as a constructivist-a social constructivist, not a radical constructivist. What this meant was that I enjoyed the notion that reality is a construction. It doesn't exist except when and as social groups decide it does. Everything is political. Everything has its own economy.

This is well and good until you go face to face with some of the realities that some of your students are dealing with. These realities are hard. They are absolutely NOT socially driven or constructed. The are not socially mediated, nor are they socially mediatable (despite the language one can apply to situations, and the extreme euphemisms or "newspeak" that is invoked.

I cut my teeth on George Batailles' *Tears of Eros*. I used Antonin Artaud's *The Theatre of Cruelty* as a point of departure of countless essays and critical perspectives. Jose Ortega y Gasset's *The Dehumanization of Art* found its way into almost everything I wrote.

Now I see the works as incredibly arrogant and insensitive - not the ideas, but the application of them. The best way to approach them is as extended metaphors.

So - I blithely invoke torture, dehumanization, and the spectacle of death as every day terms to express a kind of coded way to talk about how we try to reconnect emotion, body, and symbols (language).

Fine. But how does it play in Dubuque? Or at Bagram AFB in Afghanistan, or in Baghdad?

For the person who is or has been in harm's way, the language and approach are painful, offensive, insensitive, or worse.

So, what happens when the professor's habitual invocation of the most shocking of metaphors to illustrate very pedestrian concerns, hits the consciousness of the active-duty military student who spends days and weeks in medical evacuation helicopters, trying to keep gravely wounded 18-year-olds alive?

They tend to speak in understatement. Their language is terse, sometimes ribald, always to the point.

What we see is an automatic dysjunct - a disconnect that is amazingly painful and counterproductive.

How does one close the gap? My personal feeling is that the responsibility rests on the professor and his or her institution. They need to get on board and speak the same language, or at least develop listening skills that will be effective in both online and hybrid courses.

In my opinion, the shortest way to success is to reground the learning strategies in lived experience. This is a situated approach, and it brings the course objectives back in focus, rather than losing one's way in the dark wood of one-sided instruction, activities, and learning approach.

It requires flexibility - but the first step on the way is to listen, and to respond to real (not invented) needs.

In Extremus Distance Education Success Hinges on Enhanced Learner Autonomy

The sergeant major is sitting in a "hardened" tent somewhere in or near harm's way. The online element of the course is accessed via satellite connection. In about 2 months, the student will go to a one-week course held on base in Europe for a face-to-face component. A project manager for the Red Cross is sitting in a FEMA trailer in the Hurricane Katrina-ravaged bayous of rural southern Louisiana. Meanwhile, a newly commissioned officer in the Coast Guard is lying on his bunk (rack), his HP handheld computer in hand, browsing through the leadership course he is taking. He reads the course objectives, listens to lectures, watches a slide show and brief movies - all on his handheld computer the size of a Palm Pilot.

The delivery methods range from interactive, web-based formats, to content delivered via a chip inserted into a handheld, in a way that reminds one of a game. However, what remains constant is the fact that the courses are administered at a distance, often under very awkward, harsh, or disruptive conditions.

What are the key secrets of success? Things are not always what they seem. Perhaps one thinks it's all about a high-tech presentation, and Hollywood-produced videos. Perhaps one thinks it's all about developing realistic, video-game-based simulations.

These are good components, but what is most important is learner autonomy. The distance learner - in a 100% distance course, or a hybrid - succeeds when he or she can exercise autonomy.

What do we mean by learner autonomy?
--Options for learner self-direction
--Learner activities can be done independently
--Learners have the opportunity to be self-starters

Certain conditions must be satisfied in order for learner autonomy to be at all possible. What are they?

--Learners must be able to use the technology (the hardware as well as the software. This applies now more than ever with handheld devices, portable data devices, etc.).

--The learning management system must be understandable, and there should be help that is available on-demand.

--Instructions for administrative tasks should be easy to find and use (online registration, online payment, etc.).

--The order of tasks, instructional activities, rubrics, etc. should be organized in a way that is easy to find and follow.

--The course objectives should be flexible enough to allow the learner to adapt them and make connections between one's own goals and course content and objectives.

--The course should be designed in such a way that one can take course content, organize it, and use it as a point of departure for generalizations and meta-cognitive tasks.

--The course design should be developed in a way that when learners identify "holes in scaffolding," they can go back and fill in the gaps.

Accessibility Standards: Guidelines for Web Content Developers

This article focuses on disabled e-learners and provides guidelines for developing web-based courses that are accessible by users operating in contexts that are different than one's own.

In 1999, the World Wide Web Consortium (W3C) published "Web Content Accessibility Guidelines" to help developers make web content accessible to people with disabilities. The standards are general. It's been five years since these guidelines were published, and their concepts can be applied to online course development.

Characteristics of users and conditions:

- Users may have low vision and may have difficulty with certain fonts. San-serif fonts are usually more advisable, and the size should not be tied to a specific pixel or point size. Web editing programs such as Dreamweaver MX allow one to choose relative size, which is scalable in most web browsers. Internet Explorer is still most amenable to screen reading software and hardware.
- Users may be in conditions of low light, using black and white monitors, or in conditions of high background noise.
- Users may not be able to see, hear, have range of motion, or be able to cognitively or physically process certain types of information. As a result, they may be using certain software and hardware as screen readers and voice synthesizers.
- Users may have a screen that displays text only, and not graphics or multimedia files.
- Users may be in a context that requires them to use their hands, ears, or eyes for another task. For example, they may be driving or operating in a loud environment.

- Users may not fluently speak or read the language in which the web document is written. They may be using translation software to create a version in a different language.
- Users may have an internet connection that is slow, or has restrictions on it, such as firewalls or other security elements that make certain applications, such as java, javascript, or flash inoperative.
- Users may not be able to use a keyboard or mouse. They may be using software or hardware that allows them to send commands to the computer in alternative ways.
- Users may have internet accessibility issues having to do with browsers and operating systems. They may have different operating systems or browsers, or the version they have may be incompatible.
- Users may have difficulty reading or comprehending text.

The following are drawn from W3C guidelines, with a brief comment on how they apply to developing web-based courses:

Provide equivalent alternatives to auditory and visual content.

- Use alt tags with your graphics. This will allow an individual to mouse over a graphic and obtain a description. One can also present the material so that it is available through Braille readers (visually impaired), synthesized speech (visually impaired, cognitive/reading difficulties), and visually displayed text (hearing impaired).
- The text must convey the same information as the function or purpose as the image, as well as descriptive content.
- Providing non-text equivalents (pictures, videos, audio) of the text can be useful for nonreaders and other users who have difficulty reading.

Don't rely on color alone

- Remember that many users may be downloading to black-and-white displays, such as those found in certain devices such as cell phones or personal data assistants. Further, some may have difficulty differentiating colors, particularly if they are vision impaired. Thus, contrast is important. Do not use color alone to highlight or emphasize important content. Place consistent text to indicate headings and titles.

Provide context and orientation navigation.

- A consistent design and layout of the document will allow users to locate themselves within the web page, and to follow the proper sequence of events.
- Explain the navigation scheme and the editorial conventions.
- Navigation guides can consist of titles displayed immediately next to or over the content. This should be consistent.
- Group related links.
- If potentially confusing formats are used, be sure to orient them so that the reader can gain an understanding of the sequence and organization. Avoid complex image maps. Other problematic elements include scroll bars, side-by-side frames, or graphics / icons that guide sighted users.
- Include detailed orientation, which could consist of a paragraph description of each element. For example, titles of sections could contain a description.
- Use meta-tags to provide overview information about the content included on a page.

Provide clear navigation mechanisms.

- Establish editorial conventions and be consistent.
- Mark up documents with appropriate structural elements.
- Avoid tables or headers to accomplish certain effects.
- Remember that older browsers may not render the elements in the way desired.

Ensure that documents are clear and simple.

- Use clear sentences and avoid complex constructions. This benefits individuals with low vision as well as those with cognitive disabilities.
- Supplement text with graphic or auditory presentations where they will facilitate comprehension.
- Divide large blocks of information into smaller, more easily understood groups
- Associate labels explicitly with their controls.
- Identify the "natural language" of the document and tag it in html (for readers and translations software).
- Use clear and simple language. This will benefit individuals for whom the "natural language" is not the first language.
- Avoid spellings of compound words that result in mispronunciations by speech synthesizing software. An example is the word "homepage" -- that is pronounced as "hommipadj" by some readers. Spelling the word as two separate words, "home page," solves the problem.

Create websites that transform gracefully.

- Graceful transformation refers to the way that various readers and accommodation software and hardware possibilities.
- Make sure that the trigger scripts event handlers are input device independent.
- Make sure that the trigger scripts work when scripts are turned off, blocked, or rendered inoperable by security software or possible conflicts with other programs.
- Avoid causing the screen to flicker. This can trigger epileptic seizures in some people.
- Avoid moving content in the page, or allow the user to freeze content.
- Do not create periodically self-refreshing pages. Auto-refresh may create movement, or flickers.
- Do not use markups to redirect pages automatically. Instead, use server-side programming to redirect.

Ensure user control of time-sensitive content changes.

- Indicate when an update is available and provide a method to update.
- Avoid pop-ups or new screens. Some readers will not be able to follow them, or they may be using a script that is not readable (java applets, etc.).
- Avoid disorienting the users by requiring complex navigation, or spawned windows.

Developing Online Courses for the Visually Impaired

E-learners with low vision often find that online programs do not accommodate their needs. Departments often have an incomplete understanding of disability rights legislation. Hardware and software solutions exist, as well as web design that can assure compliance.

Low vision accessibility affects an increasing number of people as the American population ages. What is not often factored in, however, is the surge of individuals with low vision due to chronic disease, such as diabetes, and to war injuries in Afghanistan and Iraq, which some have estimated to be as high as 5,000 people. For disabled veterans, returning to school to pursue an education is a priority, and is often a part of a rehabilitation plan to enter a new career. For aging or chronically ill individuals, obtaining education and training online can also be a part of the pursuit of a second career.

Disability Rights Legislation:

In May 2002, the United States Department of Justice's Civil Rights Division published "A Guide to Disability Rights Laws." It provides an overview of the key legislation enacted since the pivotal Rehabilitation Act of 1973, which took a first step in assuring that individuals with a disability in the United States have access to employment, commerce, and education.

In brief, the Rehabilitation Act of 1973 made it illegal for any program or activity receiving Federal funding to fail to provide access to individuals with disabilities. It would be quite difficult to find a program or activity that does not receive federal financial assistance, even if they receive it indirectly.

Rehabilitation Act of 1973: Section 504
"Section 504 states that "no qualified individual with a disability in the United States shall be excluded from, denied the

benefits of, or be subjected to discrimination under" any program or activity that either receives Federal financial assistance or is conducted by any Executive agency or the United States Postal Service."
http://www.usdoj.gov/crt/ada/cguide.htm#anchor65610

Rehabilitation Act of 1973: Section 508
"Section 508 establishes requirements for electronic and information technology developed, maintained, procured, or used by the Federal government. Section 508 requires Federal electronic and information technology to be accessible to people with disabilities, including employees and members of the public."
(http://www.usdoj.gov/crt/ada/cguide.htm#anchor65610)

§ 794d of Section 508 (http://www.access-board.gov/sec508/guide/act.htm) deals specifically with electronic and information technology accessibility standards. This section created a very important provision, the "equivalent alternatives" or the "alternative means efforts," which became the method by which most agencies and institutions achieved compliance:.

"When development, procurement, maintenance, or use of electronic and information technology that meets the standards published by the Access Board under paragraph (2) would impose an undue burden, the Federal department or agency shall provide individuals with disabilities covered by paragraph (1) with the information and data involved by an alternative means of access that allows the individual to use the information and data." (The Rehabilitation Act Amendments).

Americans with Disabilities Act (ADA) of 1990: Regulations and Technical Assistance
http://www.usdoj.gov/crt/ada/publicat.htm

ADA Regulation for Title II , as printed in the Federal Register (7/26/91). The Department of Justice's regulation implementing title II, subtitle A, of the ADA which prohibits discrimination on the basis of disability in all services, programs, and activities provided to the public by State and local governments, except public transportation services." (Regulations and Technical Assistance 2001).

Non-compliance can be costly. Not only must the non-compliant party remedy the situation by making the accommodations available, they can also lose government financial aid, and/or be required to stop operations until full compliance is established. ADA Title II complaints (www.usdoj.gov/crt/ada/t2cmpfrm.htm .) are filed by individuals or governmental agencies.

Hardware:

The following websites provide information about hardware that can be used with a personal computer to allow increased functionality and access for individuals with low vision.

IBM Accessibility Center -- http://www-306.ibm.com/able/ This is an excellent page which provides links to many commercial products and services, ranging from text readers to guidelines for web developers. There are links to consultancy services which will evaluate client websites and provide customized programming and modification. This could be perfect for an institution needing an effective and timely return to compliance, although it could prove to be costly.

Freedom Scientific -- http://www.freedomscientific.com/ JAWS for Windows ® -- (screen-reader software) http://www.freedomscientific.com/fs_products/software_jaws.asp JAWS is one of the most popular screen readers for personal computers. It includes software, a speech synthesizer, and a sound card to "read" the text on a screen to the low-vision user.

Adaptive Technology Resource Centre: http://www.utoronto.ca/atrc/ Technology Glossary: http://www.utoronto.ca/atrc/reference/tech/techgloss.html The Adaptive Technology Resource Center offers information, workshops, and programs to help individuals with disabilities use technology to gain access, and it helps institutions develop programs that are accessible to individuals with disabilities.

Eyewear -- Overview from the Low Vision Centers of Indiana (http://www.eyeassociates.com/lowsysms.htm): This website provides a catalogue of low vision solutions, ranging from goggles, to screen readers.

National Center for Accessible Media (http://ncam.wgbh.org/) The National Center for Accessible Media, (NCAM), is a division of WBGH Boston, a 50-year-old institution of public broadcasting. It has been a leader in the development of media accessible technologies, including being a pioneer in captioning. Its radio, television, and webcast programs are enjoyed worldwide.

Software:

The following websites provide information about software that can be used with a personal computer to allow increased functionality and access for the blind or vision-impaired. These include screen readers, "talking books," and software that scales and/or converts fonts.

Microsoft Accessibility -- http://www.microsoft.com/enable/

Resource Guide for Individuals with Vision Difficulties and Impairment -- http://www.microsoft.com/enable/guides/vision.aspx

Digital Talking Book -- Section 508 standards: http://www.access-board.gov/sec508/talking-book/intro-eng.htm

Download gh PLAYER http://www.ghbraille.com/playerdownload.html

Design Guidelines:

The following websites provide information about how web design can help provide access to individuals with low vision.

Guidelines include areas such as the use of color, types and sizes of fonts, use of style sheets, convertability, use of graphics, and more.

World Wide Web Consortion (W3C): <u>Web Content Accessibility Guidelines 1.0</u> : http://www.w3.org/TR/WAI-WEBCONTENT/

American Council of the Blind -- http://www.acb.org/

Designing Web Usability: http://www.usability.com/

The Business of Distance and Flexible Courses and Programs

Business Trends and E-Learning: Affiliates, Monetizing, Direct Navigation

What does it take to achieve solid, fast-paced growth in an e-learning organization? It's not just about building courses, recruiting students, or containing costs. It's also about generating new revenue streams, which may include establishing affiliate relationships, monetizing websites through advertising and reciprocal relationships, and acquiring "valuable real estate" (domains) in order to monetize them, then sell as "type-in" direct navigation domains. Needless to say, it's important to be perceived as maintaining academic excellence as you build student and revenue bases. Nevertheless, there are exciting new ways that have been newly legitimized by investment banking firms for organizations (including e-learning organizations) to establish relationships and to market and promote products, services, and approaches.

Affiliate Marketing

Affiliate software has evolved tremendously since 2001, and during the last year, new programs and Internet capabilities have emerged that allow smaller institutions to harness the power of a whole new level of the Internet.

While the massive programs (Google Adsense, Yahoo Commission Junction, Amazon) still make sense, it's becoming easier to affiliate with small, independent, yet high-traffic sites. The end result is that the owners of medium and low-traffic weblogs, websites, and podcasts promote programs for a small fee based on clicks, leads, or commissions. Or, alternatively, there are new opportunities to affiliate with providers of the services your clients want and need and to receive commissions - all in a completely seamless manner.

Some individuals at educational institutions may cringe and say that this approach is really crass and tacky. However, they fail to keep in mind that state and private colleges and universities have been doing this for years, but in a way that is not usually acknowledged.

For example, stroll through the student union of an average college campus, look around you and observe what there is to purchase. You will see florists, travel agencies, fast food, copy centers, class rings, cell phone providers, credit card company sign-up tables, book stores, and branded clothing or gift items. The college will receive a percentage of sales from virtually ever transaction done. It is not viewed as selling out. Instead, this is a viable partnership.

What has not been perfected is how these commercial relationships and partnerships function best for online institutions. I would venture to say that it is different for each institution, and that it is important to not seek a generic solution, but to take the time to identify needs, constituencies, and products to align them **in the most appropriate way.**

Examples include the following:

Personal Affiliate Manager (PAM), developed by George Cain. (shareware)

http://www.sharewareconnection.com/personal-affiliate-manager.htm (from the website: *Personal Affiliate Manager is all you need to organize, manage and report on all of your personal affiliate site subscriptions. Keep all of the your various affiliate site logins, URL link codes, commissions and profits all within one simple program.*)

Affiliate Network Solution, developed by Pilot Group. Net. (shareware)
http://www.sharewareconnection.com/affiliate-network-solution.htm
PilotGroup.Net: http://www.pilotgroup.net/index.php
(from the website: *The most effective marketing tool to earn money on-line. Simple and easy-to-set-up program. The design can be easily changed to suit you. Thousands of products, partners, and ads. A full-service advertising network. Affiliates can check their statistics and get ads through a special page. Includes detailed sales and click-through statistics. Fixed and non-fixed price products. Both automatic and manual sales approval. Powerful payout control. Comprise Owner Admin*

Area with many features. HTML Code Generator for affiliate setup. Powerful organization tool and business manager for your online business.)

Stats Remote, developed by Network 24/7 (shareware)
http://www.sharewareconnection.com/statsremote.htm
Statsremote home: http://www.statsremote.com/
This program has a "FOUR COWS" rating at 2cows.com, and is a 2004 XBiz Award winner. *(from the website: StatsRemote is automatic stats-checking software for affiliates and pay-per-click search-engine webmasters. It checks the statistics of your affiliate programs and pay-per-click search engines automatically, with no need to manually log in to each stats area, as the software does it all for you. StatsRemote reads and displays your hits, sales, and money directly from the stats areas of the affiliate programs and PPC search engines, so you have all the numbers right in front of you. In addition, you can add custom income and expenses (server bills and traffic purchases, for example). StatsRemote can check your stats as often as every 15 minutes and displays all your numbers and a forecast for the current month, or daily, previous, or year-to-date stats, in one interface.)*

Website Monetization.

I've also been investigating the opportunities that exist with monetizing websites, and domain sponsoring, in order to untangle hype from reality.

To be honest, I find the concept of filling a webpage with links to advertisers (without any real content) to be sort of repugnant. I know that I do not like landing on domain names filled with links when I misspell a domain name. For example, check out http://www.yahho.com/ and you'll see what I'm talking about.

One of the software solutions that helps individuals with domain sponsor businesses build links is Alstrasoft.com
http://www.alstrasoft.com/domains.htm

Companies such as Chitika will help a person develop a monetized website for a share of the ad revenues. In this case, it is 60%. They also have a product, e-minimalls, which can help drive ad and referral revenue. Billed as the "leader in impulse marketing," chitika.com has (I am assuming) spent a great deal of time figuring out what makes people click. I think they have my number. https://chitika.com/index.php Actually, I know they have my number.

I personally question how often content-less sites get picked up by search engines, primarily google. On the other hand, generating traffic is a multi-dimensional art, which is all the more complicated by blogs, podcasts, and other syndicated content. I have seen blogs (particularly celebrity-based blogs) that seem to be little more than placeholders for affiliate-program ad links. I suppose it is a matter of degree. It could be viewed as a service to provide links to related products (I certainly have discovered new products and have purchased items this way). On the other hand, no one wants to be adrift on a sea of fluff and google adsense.

The *Wall Street Journal* had an interesting article in November 2005, in which they described some of the big players in the domain name monetization business. Domain aggregators have assembled venture capital to purchase domain names - to the tune of $250 million!

Along with the new surge in investment and ad revenue, a shift in attitudes has occurred:
"The business model has shifted," said Matt Bentley, chief executive of domain broker Sedo.com LLC, which managed the sale of website.com for $750,000 this year. "The fact that it is moving from individuals to larger corporations … represents a legitimization of the domain-name industry." For years, the industry had a less-than-rosy reputation because many domain owners dealt in "cyber-squatting," registering names associated with famous brands in hopes of selling them to a big company at a hefty price, which fueled legal squabbles. (Thanks to Web Ads, Some Find New Money in Domain Names, WSJ, 17 Nov. 2005)

The shift was a hot topic at a recent ICANN meeting, where the debate about parked domains continues. Joi Ito wrote an interesting post in in CircleID.com in December 2005 about the practice and some of the issues:

http://www.circleid.com/posts/the_parked_domain_monetizatio
n_business/
According to him, the "Parked Domain Monetization Business"
is making it easier for squatters to operate, and more difficult for
individuals and businesses to purchase the domain name they
want. The analogy used these days is real estate. Hot "type-in"
type domain names are viewed as valuable virtual real estate.

On the other hand, there are a number of nuances, and I still
think that it is possible that monetization without content may
go away sometime in the future, particularly if google and other
search engines do not acknowledge pages that consist only of
ads and links.

Direct Navigation

The other issue, the concept of "direct navigation" is very
problematic to me. I suppose there is something to it, but my
preliminary research into the subject is at odds with what the
apologists claim. They describe direct navigation in the
following way: "Simply put, Direct Navigation is finding the
information you're looking for without using a search engine, a
directory of sites, or clicking on a link from another site."
http://www.directnavigationmarket.com/ According to the
website, "type in traffic" is natural traffic, because there is an
affinity to the product. To rely on search engines and search
engine-driven traffic is ultimately futile, because conditions
always change.

The implications for the e-learning organization are multiple.
First, it means that there is more competition for sites you may
wish to purchase. It also means that your bookstore will be
competing with millions of other sites that will offer the same
products, but possibly at a lower price. Eventually, courses and
software could be sold in this way (not only products). Certainly
many colleges (not just the University of Phoenix) have
aggressively embraced affiliate marketing, which means,
indirectly, they are participating in the direct navigation market
and the parked domain monetization business, since their ads
may show up there.

The issues are complex and worth exploring. For now, I'm content to explore and try to keep up with the trends.

Communities of Practice: Role of Taxonomies and Classification Schemes

It had been a hard day in the e-learning trenches, and online English composition faculty member Jill Deleuze was looking for some place to share her pain. She logged into the College of Ste. Justine English Department's page, and perused the discussion boards and links. It was a remarkably jejune experience. There was the same 3-week-old discussion thread about exam procedures, and a set of links to software she did not have time to learn. One thread led her, unexpectedly, to a set of audio files for the *Da Vinci Code*. She listened while clicking on the links to the various textbook websites and an online grammar review. This was more like it, she thought. Unfortunately, there were only four links to e-learning content, activities, or objects, none which tied directly to her courses.

It occurred to Dr. Deleuze that there may be a community of users out there who had developed resources she could use in her English classes. Was there an up-to-date MERLOT? Something with objects she could use with Learn-O-Rama, the new learning management system that Ste. Justine's information technology team developed, would be ideal. Despite the IT team's enthusiasm, and platform's accolades at e-LearnTech's national convention, the faculty and staff of Ste. Justine insisted that Learn-O-Rama was not very friendly. One issue that made it unfriendly was that it required rigid SCORM compliancy. Jill sighed. She loved "Grammar Bytes" at http://www.chompchomp.com/, but because all objects had to be hosted on the Ste. Justine server, she could not use it.

Frustrated, she typed a quick e-mail to the chair of the department, Dr. Pantagruel. It was an exercise in futility. Dr. Pantagruel was in complete agreement, but they were a choir of two. Was there any way to reach across the entire campus and solve some of the pressing problems that Learn-O-Rama presented? Was there any way to share objects and e-tivities?

Logging onto bloglines (http://www.bloglines.com/), she read the latest feeds, then clicked on the links to her favorite blogs. Glancing over some promising headlines, she clicked on "Projects and Collaborations" link to Stephen Downes http://www.downes.ca/projects.htm. She read a few items on the topic of collaborative learning, then posted what she considered a brilliantly ironic remark about tangential communication, then went on to the next link.

That was the main problem with all these collaborations, Jill thought. There was a lack of direct communication. Sure, sometimes people actually answered a question, but more often, the responses were tangential.

Community through groups and discussion boards.

She thought of the google.groups she had joined. Although they were bulky, they were a great improvement over the old "usenet" and alt.net discussion groups. Jill had recently joined the "Historical Romance Book Group." It wasn't that she knew anything about historical romances. The concrete topic – a virtual book club – seemed to be one of the few places she had ever found a group of people who stayed on topic.

There were a few elements she did not like, however. One was the idea of a moderator. Despite the claims of researchers such as Salmon (2002), who claimed that the key to successful e-learning and teaching was moderating the discussion board, Jill felt annoyed by the moderator. She felt inhibited, and tended to self-censor, even though she knew one reason for that was because of "comment-spamming." No one needed Viagra ads in a Historical Romance group discussion. Moderators also tended to over-control and micro-manage, which put the back in the dreaded "sage on the stage" role. In an article she read by DiRamio (2005), Jill read that research demonstrated that instructors should not inhibit collaborations by micro-managing, nor should they control the information to be disseminated.

Storing and retrieving information: The importance of taxonomies

What frustrated her most were elements that had to do with retrieval. Even if she had an idea to share, it was hard to know where to post it on a campus-wide discussion board. A clear taxonomy needed to be developed. Jill clicked on the Living Taxonomy Project (LPT) and read the mission statement developed by its visionary founder, Stacy Zemke:

The Living Taxonomy Project is a collaborative effort aimed at creating a global set of open source, standards-based taxonomies for education. The purpose of these taxonomies will be to provide a free cataloging structure for the collection and sharing of education materials around the world. We will be appending new taxonomies on a regular basis and invite our users to add edit these taxonomies as well as suggest or create new ones.

In this case, a taxonomy referred to a classification system. Certain assumptions and questions had to be worked out, and collaboration / discussion was the best way to do it. For example, are taxonomies developed around an alphabetized list that is designed to be all-inclusive? Or, do the taxonomies and the sub-divisions emerge from causal relationships, or families?

Stacy Zemke had addressed many of those questions. She also challenged people to think about issues in a new way. Jill was most intrigued by the film genre taxonomy, as well as math taxonomies. Could this approach work?

Taxonomies are best worked out in the natural sciences -- Jill thought of mineralogy as a good example. Igneous rocks are classified by texture, normative (suite-- this has to do with the way the minerals were formed), and modal (depends on the relative amounts of certain rock-forming minerals). Taxonomies could be confusing and conflicting. Yet, they were a great way to get to understand a thing in an in-depth way and from multiple perspectives.

Threaded discussions (topics not clearly spelled out – need taxonomy). How would she go about classifying the topics? DiRamio (2005) suggested that the way that information is shared should be user-driven. Students should be able to assume leadership roles in collaborations. Likewise, faculty and staff should be able to organize information. It should not be technology or interface driven. Instead, the technology should work for the users.

All text, no objects. Jill knew that her courses could be much better if she had more learning objects, and "e-tivities." They should encourage engagement. But, she had no way to obtain or share.

Perhaps she would approach Dean Bataille about developing a shared e-space where individuals could organize objects. Would these ideas work in a university setting? Could they develop a place where they could share objects, and activities?

Even more importantly, the faculty and staff could be given guidance in how to use the objects through effective training and online guides. What constitutes an effective instructional strategy? Jill thought back to when she first started developing websites. Her first one had a lot in common with Angelfire's "The World's Worst Website" - http://www.angelfire.com/super/badwebs/

Jill hoped that she did not commit the same errors when she used online learning objects. She knew that she should keep the outcome in mind, but it was important to let others take a leadership role so that both the outcome and the way to achieve the outcome, were fluid, flexible, and meaningful.

Bibliography and Useful Resources

DiRamio, D.. (2005). Measuring online community. Online Classroom. June 2005. 2-4.

Gorard, S. & Selwyn, N. (1999). Switching on the learning society? -- Questioning the role of technology in widening participation in lifelong learning. Journal of Education Policy. 14. 523-534.

Govindasamy, T. (2002). Successful implementation of e-Learning. Pedagogical considerations. ScienceDirect-The Internet and Higher Education, 4, 287-299.

Living Taxonomy Project. http://www.livingtaxonomy.org

Orrill, C. H. (2002). Supporting online PBL: design considerations for supporting distributed problem solving. Distance Education, 23, 42-57.

Pavey, J., Garland, S. W. (2004). The integration and implementation of a range of 'e-tivities' to enhance students' interaction and learning. Innovations in Education and Teaching International, 41, 305-315.

Salmon, G. (2002). E-Moderating: the key to teaching and learning online. London: Kogan Page.

Taxonomies of Practice: Learning Object Repositories in E-Learning

The College of Ste. Justine had decided to develop its own learning object repository (LOR) for faculty members across the campus. The idea sounded good, but geology professor Horst Charendon was annoyed. The proposed classification system, or taxonomy, was completely irrelevant to his purposes, he argued. Debbie Virtue, Ste. Justine's LOR project director, tried to maintain her patience.

"We are using google desktop search capabilities. Taxonomies are obsolete. Just type in a search term," Virtue said.

"Well, maybe that's okay for some learning objects, but it doesn't work at all where the discipline utilizes alternative classification schemes. Using google search will result in incomplete results. Some data will be invisible," retorted Charendon.

"That's impossible," said Virtue. She truly believed in the power of google.

"I understand where you're coming from, but as we tag the objects, or have information attached to them, if they are in one classification system, they may not be in the others," said Charendon.

"Igneous petrology is a case in point," he said. "We use three different classification schemes to describe igneous rocks."

"Each rock has three different names? I don't believe it. Wouldn't that lead to chaos?" asked Virtue.

Charendon described igneous classification schemes, or taxonomies.

Taxonomy / Classification Scheme 1. Igneous rock Color-

Texture.

Taxonomy / Classification Scheme 2: Igneous rock Modal classification classifies igneous rocks on the relative abundance of five minerals they may contain.

Taxonomy / Classification Scheme 3. The Normative classification arranges igneous rocks into suites, each suite characterized by a particular chemistry.

Another similar challenge is with sedimentary rocks; in particular, carbonates, including limestone and dolomite.

"As much as we would like to use a different approach, or consolidate everything into a single taxonomy, we are prisoners of practice," he said. "It is not just something that happens at Ste. Justine. It happens everywhere."

"Do you think the same thing might apply to other areas of endeavor?" asked Virtue.

"Quite possibly. It is definitely the case with carbonate rocks," said Charendon.

"I still maintain that a google-type site LOR search will work," maintained Virtue, perversely.

"No. It won't. You will just get incomplete coverage. Or, just one term instead of all three for the same rock," said Charendon.

Horst Charendon and Debbie Virtue left the room. The atmosphere was definitely frosty.

A week went by. Virtue asked the Ste. Justine LOR committee to start investigating taxonomies, partly in an attempt to one-up Charendon.

In doing so, she made a discovery: The Living Taxonomy Project. http://www.livingtaxonomy.org

Forgetting her desire to humiliate him, Virtue called up Charendon. She was excited about her "find."

"Horst, you'll never believe what I found! Stacy Zemke, who is the founder of the Living Taxonomy Project, is developing a revolutionary way to accommodate competing classification schemes, without having to resort to a site search for key words," she said. Horst listened quietly, rather in shock about her change in attitude.

"How is this different from what Rory McGreal has described in his work on ontologies and taxonomies (www.downes.ca/files/CEN.doc) It is being hosted on Stephen Downes' website (http://www.downes.ca)?" asked Charendon.

"I consider what the Living Taxonomy Project is doing to be a "taxonomy of practice" rather than a definitive retrieval system," said Virtue.

She went on to describe the possibilities of classification. A classification system could be descriptive. Alternatively, it could focus on function (rather than form), or, it could be about origin or provenance. All depended on the practice.

"Words are inherently slippery. Think about what post-structuralists and deconstructivists have maintained - Lakoff, Derrida, etc. They claim that the word itself creates the meaning, and that taxonomies are simply agreed-upon conventions," Dean Pantagruel was eavesdropping and could not resist chiming in.

"That makes my head swim," said Virtue.

"Well, it should," said Dean Pantagruel. "The multiplicity of interpretative possibility has been around since St. Augustine and Poetics."

"What does Alan Levine of cogdogblog (http://jade.mcli.dist.maricopa.edu) have to say? I really respect his work," said Dean Pantagruel.

"According to Levine, it's a very contentious issue. (http://jade.mcli.dist.maricopa.edu/cdb/2005/01/25/what-were/)," said Virtue.

"And, speaking of Contentious (http://blog.contentious.com/) , what does Amy Gahran have to say?" continued Pantagruel.

"She tends to be inclusive rather than exclusive. I would say that her taxonomies are referential and built on allusions or links," said Virtue.

"Cognitive dissonance!" barked Dean Pantagruel. "The more voices, the better. And, speaking of Cognitive Dissonance, I like what Nate Lowell has to say (http://durandus.com/blog/)"

Dusk was falling on the College of Ste. Justine. The ivy-covered clock tower loomed over the shadowed campus. As the campus sank into darkness, a full moon rose and the bare branches of trees clawed the impotent sky. From the bowels of the brick and cornice building that housed the computer center and the new server dedicated to Learn-O-Rama, Ste. Justine's proprietary learning management system, a piercing female shriek rent the skies.

"Peccatores, Ut nobis parcas, Ut nobis indulgeas, Ut ad veram paenitentiam nos perducere digneris." There was a long pause and then a howl. "Through our taxonomies we know our deeds and we seek forgiveness!!"

The Cottage Industry Problem in Online Education

The friendly learning management software, or "LMS" rep promised a scalable enterprise solution that, together with an Oracle database, would result in a virtual campus that would run itself. It was a scene right out of *R.U.R.: Rossum's Universal Robots.* The only worry was that the computer would come alive a la *Terminator* and try to take over. Ah, if only that were true!

Quite the reverse is true on most campuses. Instead of a sleek, smoothly functioning factory, what usually results is more akin to a cottage industry or, worse, a sweatshop.

From the outside, everything appears to be integrated and automated. One would never suspect that each step of the online process is accompanied by laborious piecework, and that it is not possible to expand the program, or to control quality of content, services, instruction, or access. In order to detect where bottlenecks are occurring, and hand-crafted, cottage industry piecework takes place, it is necessary to conduct a thorough review of the process.

The characteristics of cottage industry in online programs, beginning with course development, and progressing through administrative and academic services, include the following:

1. *Processes Knitted Together by Hand.* Instead of seamless integration of services, there pieces in the process that involve faxing information, taking it over the phone, or processing printed forms, with resulting duplications of effort, bottlenecks, and time-intensive work.

2. *Facades of Automation.* The online forms are not true forms that integrate into a database where the information is easily retrievable. Instead, the information comes in and must be re-entered by hand into a database program.

3. *No Division of Labor.* This is probably the most important aspect of the process, and the key to improving efficiency and providing a uniform product of high quality. Specialization of labor is involved, after a close analysis of the work flow, tasks, and procedures.

4. *Ergonomically Incorrect.* The average workspace or lab is often ergonomically incorrect, resulting in potential physical injuries, including carpal tunnel syndrome.

5. *Too Many Repetitive Tasks.* Although specialization is important, and appropriate division of labor, it is possible to push this concept to unhealthy extremes. The worst is perhaps the call center atmosphere -- the university has been turned into a giant call center, which reminds one of a medical insurance claim processing center rather than an institution of higher learning.

6. *No Integration of Tasks, No Sense of Flow.* In addition to failing to analyze tasks and coordinate them, institutions often fail to properly integrate databases, tasks, and/or responsibilities. As a result, information does not flow to the proper places, and it has to be submitted multiple times.

7. *No Uniformity of Process.* It is important to develop procedures and to follow them -- even in other parts of the college. This allows training to be developed and depth / breadth of personnel so that surges in volume can be accommodated, and a truly scalable solution can be developed.

8. *Unnecessary Intermediaries.* If there are intermediaries, they should serve a real function (eArmyU, for example) that cannot be otherwise replicated. Even when intermediaries are necessary, it is important to develop policies and procedures to avoid the "high-centering" phenomenon (the work gets hung up and does not progress past the intermediary) or the "ping pong effect" where the tasks bounce from one intermediary unit to another, without resolution.

9. *Tasks Not Classified, Task "Families" Not Developed.* In developing appropriate division of labor and specialization, it is

vital to analyze the tasks and classify them. Thus classified, "task families" can be developed and individuals with "like" activities can be grouped together. This helps allocate tasks for maximum efficiency.

There are other issues and problems that hinge upon human relationships and leadership decisions and policies. These are dealt with in Part 2 of this series.

Solving the "Cottage Industry" Problem in E-Learning Programs

Major process and production reviews are key to eliminating the bottlenecks, burnout, errors, gaps in service, non-scalability, poor quality control, unresponsiveness to needs of users that typify the "cottage industry problem" in e-learning programs. Specialization and division of labor are not actually employed. Most institutions are unaware that what masquerades as a streamlined, high-tech "factory" is, in fact, a series of discrete, unconnected silos, where information is hoarded, valuable instructional technologists are hand-inputting what should be an automated process, content and learning objects are reinvented unnecessarily or trapped in legacy applications, and increases in volume cannot be easily accommodated.

Division of Labor. Perhaps the most dominant characteristic of the cottage industry problem in e-learning programs is faulty division of labor. Either there is very little division of labor, and one person is hand-crafting the entire course or program by himself or herself, or there is too much division of labor, and individual talent is being wasted by reducing tasks to mind-numbingly boring data entry, or by developing elements for "legacy" systems that are not object oriented.

Coordination and Sharing Instead of Siloing. This may seem a matter of common sense, but it is truly amazing how often it takes place. Instead of coordinating, sharing, and re-using objects, multi-use items (including logos and learning objects), departments often develop their own. This is a class example of "reinventing the wheel," which leads not only to inefficiency, but also to territoriality, "not invented here" syndrome," negative rivalry, secretiveness, and information hoarding. Leadership must step in and take a firm position, and actively defuse rivalry and suspicion so that people will be in a positive frame of mind and able to live outside their silos. It is important to keep in mind that silos were created for a reason. Silos protect, preserve, and camouflage. They are the natural way of conducting business when the organizational culture is typified by a feeling of vulnerability and outside threat, and individuals feel a need to barricade themselves against losses of revenue, information, personnel, or influence. An organizational restructuring is often necessary in order to make coordination a reality. The flow of information and activities should be clearly mapped out, with a diagram that everyone understands.

Work Flow Analysis. Finding out what work is being done and who really does the work is not always an easy task, particularly if individuals believe that their job performance could be evaluated, and the jobs that they have could be eliminated. For that reason, it is vital to conduct a work flow analysis in more than one way. The first analysis can consist of evaluation instruments, with an overt analysis with a combination of self-assessment and self-description, simultaneously with an assessment by the supervisor of the processes, staff competencies, and sequences of tasks. The second analysis is more "stealth" and involves "shadowing" an applicant or an actively enrolled student as their files progress through the system; and, by tracking what goes on in the actual development of a curriculum, course, or course template. Once the flow is defined, it is important identify the following:

1. Where and when does work "ping pong" (bounce around from one person to another, unproductively;
2. Where and when does work "double back" or "circle" -- instead of moving forward, it moves back in the process;
3. Where do work processes funnel and hit "pinch points"? Once identified, it should be first priority to add additional staff in order to eliminate pinch points, bottlenecks, and funnels.

Task Families Identified. By assigning tasks to "task families," it is possible to cluster the work, and to assign specialists to related tasks within a family. This is at the heart of specialization and division of labor.

Task Responsibilities Identified. Rivalry and turf wars often result when more than one person has been assigned responsibility for the same task. This can result in conflicting instructions, frustration, and poor morale. Clear lines of responsibility should be established and communicated.

Tasks Assigned. Assigning tasks should be made with an eye to the overall sequence of events and flow. Further, even though there may be one person who is more adept at handling certain tasks, the tasks should be assigned with future needs and potential growth in mind. Assigning all the tasks to the most qualified person leads to silo formation and bottlenecks. Tasks should be distributed, with scalability in mind.

Task Frequencies Determined. Inefficiency is often caused when poor time management is employed, and tasks are conducted at too high a frequency. Instead, the tasks should have a sequence, and a schedule -- not too rigid (don't destroy responsiveness), but organized in a logical manner.

Inventories of Objects to be Created. In order to facilitate retrievable and reuse of reusable and sharable content objects, it is important to develop a classification scheme, together with a clear method for naming the files, and assigning them to shared, accessible archives.

Non-Variable vs. Variable Content. When developing templates for courses, and reusable objects, it is important to identify the variable and the non-variable content. Then, develop a method for clustering the variable content so that updates can be made efficiently. The more non-variable items that can be made, the better. These can be developed then reviewed and updated when deemed appropriate.

Appropriate Granularity. Content objects that are too small in size (the granularity is too fine) take too much time to organize and are difficult to manage. On the other hand, overly coarse granularity means that the entire object must be updated, and it becomes bulky and difficult to assign tasks. Coarse granularity results in silos and bottlenecks, because only one person may be able to work on the item as a whole. Once the large object is cut into smaller objects, it is easier to delegate and assign tasks.

Tasks and Objects Coordinated with Learning Objectives. It is easy for the entire organization to turn into a machine that begins to lose sight of the original reason for the various elements within the online program -- the interfaces, the databases, the online course functional elements (discussion boards, chat, grade books, etc.), course content, course interactivity. One must constantly evaluate each element in terms of learning outcomes and objectives.

Instructional Design Corresponds with Inventories. Tasks and elements should be periodically reviewed by an instructional designer to make sure that as tasks are broken out and division of labor and specialization occur, they adhere to best practices and accepted standards.

Templates, Style Sheets. Use templates and style sheets in order to be able to assign tasks to more than person, and to streamline processes.

Doing It Right the First Time. One of the most maddening "cottage industry" traits is the fact that tasks often have to be repeated and redone because they are not done correctly the first time.

LMS-Independent Learning Objects and Approaches. Institutional decisions may result in frequent changes of software solutions, including the student portals, database programs, and learning management systems. As a result, it is often necessary to migrate data and/or repurpose objects. The more platform-independent a learning object, the better. Further, some scripts may not be as functional within some platforms, and thus it is often important to minimize or use the most basic possible in terms of java, javascript, flash, or domino applet applications.

Integrative Database Solutions (Fiscal / Registration / Courses / Payroll). The same process and productivity issues that surround a learning management system also apply to integrative database solutions. It is vitally important to understand the flow of tasks, and to build in checks and balances, as well as quality control.

Focus on Scalability. Making things functional at current volumes is nice, but stopping at that point is ill advised. It is important to move ahead and think of expanding and increasing volume in terms of users, content, objects, software solutions. Scalability is the key to success.

Mentored Tasks. Training should be continuous and based on experience and need. Mentoring is perhaps one of the best ways to transfer skills, as well as operational philosophies. Mentors and new mentees should be provided with appropriate incentives and rewards.

Locus of Control: Avoid Unnecessary Intermediaries. Accountability for processes should stay as close as possible to the person who is using the elements. Introducing unnecessary intermediaries creates bottlenecks, or unexpected circumventions.

The topics listed above are vital in solving the cottage industry problem. Vigilance should be maintained, and process should be subjected to constant review and quality assurance. Ironically, division of labor and specialization taken to extremes can be, in the global environment, a contributing factor in another risk: "distributed sweatshops." Distributed sweatshops will be defined and dealt with in a future article.

Eliminating Academic Sweatshops

Academic sweatshops can be eliminated, and it can happen in ways that will actually improve efficiency and cost-effectiveness to academic units and educational content / solution providers. The next several years will see a huge change in the way that online course content is housed and administered at many colleges and universities, particularly ones that offer both online and face-to-face programs, and it will also see increasing pressure to provide maximum flexibility in terms of access and delivery modes. If the academic sweatshops, existing as they do now, are not eliminated, academic units will not be able to keep up with evolving needs.

This article is going to be brief because I can easily go on and on with this topic, and I'd rather break it up into digestible chunks.

You might ask me, "Come on, have you actually ever seen an academic sweatshop?"

The answer is, "Yes. I've seen lots of them." I've seen many of the kinds that Rob Reynolds refers to in his article on academic sweatshops, and points out that they are fairly ubiquitous. He also points out that universities have traditionally been places where labor has been exploited under the guise of "apprenticeship." Graduate students have been most shamelessly tasked with working for pennies, but assistant professors seeking tenure are often pressed into long, unrecompensed hours of labor. This is bad, and we're not even touching the issue of adjuncts.

I agree with Rob -- these are unintentional sweat shops. I would never claim that a college or a university is one of the notorious windowless shops where workers try to escape through barred windows, only to break their legs as they drop down multiple floors to hard asphalt.

Instead, you'll find the following scenarios throughout colleges, universities, educational software and instructional material providers.

Subcontractor of a subcontractor sweatshop: Somewhere along the line, you've probably wondered where all the nice learning objects, companion websites, and educational software gets developed. If you visit the corporate offices, you'll tend to find cubicles and smooth, funky desks with high-tech chairs, and even perhaps a dot.com holdover -- a daybed and pillows next to the wireless node. You marvel that such a small team can produce so much material, until someone tells you that they are helped by their "teams" or "implementing partners."

What this means is a subcontract. The subcontractor tends to be successful at obtaining contracts, and, as you well know, "opportunity clusters." This results in a need to add skilled workers, but from where? Here is where a subcontractor layer gets added. The original contract may have been generous, but each subcontract iteration results in less money to divide out to the subcontractors. Forget benefits. Forget even providing the workers with a laptop. A small subcontractor team will work a week on something that pays $1,000 gross -- unless they find there is a way to subcontract yet again -- not to India -- they're already getting to expensive -- but perhaps to a team in Pakistan or Malaysia .

I've visited software development firms in St. Petersburg , Russia , and other places, and I hear the same story everywhere. "We'll do it this one time for experience, but we're really working for nothing. Perhaps the next contract will be better." The next contract often never comes.

"The Apprentice Sweatshop" -- Graduate students in the centralized learning services office, or in departments: Years ago, when being a graduate student meant having to learn your craft by practicing on students in intro classes, or proctoring and grading tests from large lectures, the work paid poorly, but at least it was enough to cover books, tuition, and a one-bedroom apartment in a converted old Victorian house next to campus. Your job didn't require a significant investment in equipment, software, connectivity, or peripherals. Paper, pens, pencils, and a good backpack were all you needed. Now, the average graduate student is pulled into departments or in central online services units, and asked to develop or update courses and/or learning objects. Now, however, the job requires the student to have invested an average of $5,000 in simply having the tools and skills for the job. To make things worse, the graduate often receives no more than around $1,000 per month for 20 hours of work per week. Tuition waivers are often partial, and with the rapid escalation of tuition, this requires students to obtain more loans. So, ironically, the student is, in effect, subsidizing academic units through student loans.

As opposed to classic textile sweatshops, however, there is no cruel overseer or cigar-chomping robber baron at the helm. Instead, you see pale and harried department chairs hand-wringing over the budget and the need to accommodate the burgeoning demand for online courses, but without the right kind of long-term additional investment in infrastructure or staffing. At the end of the semester, when they've managed to pull off another miracle, they have managed to mask, yet again, the real circumstances. Such heroics are self-defeating.

Solitary Sweatshops: Online Adjuncts. It is my belief that in the future, semester-by-semester "hired gun" adjuncts will no longer exist. Nor will the adjunct online instructor who is reduced to spending hour upon hour in mindless and repetitive tasks, thanks to a hopelessly inadequate LMS and instructional design that mixes variable with non-variable content, requiring fiendish levels of repurposing and updating every semester.

Distance education providers will learn to appreciate their online faculty. The learning curve is just too steep and too time-intensive to train your best people, just to see them over-commit as high-quality online instructors become increasingly difficult to find. Scarcity is due to the high and ongoing investment in technology and training that is necessary for an adjunct to be successful with each generation of learning management systems, and new computers, software, and portable content delivery devices (iPods, PDAs, etc.).

What we may see are consortia of universities, colleges, or departments that will enter into a teaming agreement to share resources (course shells, LMS licensing fees, infrastructure), and which, with new economies of scale and predictable flows of income, will be able to offer 3 - 5 year renewable contracts to "contract professors." The professors will have rank, but it will have more to do with whether or not they take on mentoring and supervision duties, and the skills they master. In addition, I suspect that they will include participation in a 401(3)b retirement savings plan, plus health and dental insurance. Further, the consortia will pay for their contract professors' ongoing training, and will provide software, PDAs, and discounts on laptops.

Get Rid of Bad LMS Design. Perhaps the quickest way to a sweatshop is to use a horrible learning management system that does not archive in any sort of effective way, does not integrate with online support services (the Oracle database, or whatever is being used), does not allow group uploading of files, and requires absurd levels of clicking between screens. I won't name names, but I will say that the two biggest purveyors of learning management software should be ashamed. I won't go into detail, but if you talk to individuals who are preparing courses and course content for delivery through an LMS platform, you will hear them describe the absurd level of time-consuming and confusing tasks involved just to put together an ugly, text-only course.

Refuse to Use an LMS without Learning Object Repository Capabilities. Reusable content is the only solution. Technology's job is to make the task more efficient, not to add to and complicate the job! Desire2Learn's new version promises such capabilities. This is wonderful, and could facilitate the formation of academic consortia and teams.

Don't Silo! Share and Team. How many times have you been in a college or division-wide meeting and have heard individuals describe the tasks that are going on in their units -- identical to the ones going on in your unit. The wheel just gets reinvented -- over and over and over again. Isn't it funny how the quality never improves in such situations? Instead, each time the wheel is updated or reinvented, there are more errors and flaws.

Map Tasks, Identify Task Families, then Streamline.
Sweatshops often result because of maladaptive division of labor. Either there is not enough division of labor, and one adjunct professor is knitting everything together by hand in his or her little virtual cottage industry; or, there is too much division of labor, and it becomes tempting to get into the subcontractor chain. In order to accomplish appropriate division of labor, it's necessary to know what tasks are being done, when, and by whom. Then, after mapping and classifying tasks, identify task families, then coordinate for economies of scale.

Identify Bottlenecks, Seek to Eliminate Them. Bottlenecks occur in expected and unexpected places. For example, there may be a bottleneck in the learning services division, due to inadequate staffing and work flow analysis. There may be bottlenecks resulting from ineffectual support services (financial aid counseling, course template production, mal-integration of support services, over-reliance on outdated open-source software, etc.

Expose Facades of Automation. It is surprising how many times what seems to be an automated function is not that at all. Although a student may fill out a form online, there is no guarantee that the information is really going into a relational database where the information automatically populates itself. Instead, a human being is busy re-entering data into forms.

I feel myself starting to rave, and I think I should stop for now. This topic is inflammatory, yet it is necessary to step back and look at the processes rather than begin to rant about the evils of globalization or the corporatization of higher education. It's time to address the processes. We've already established the problem.

Distributed Communities of Practice in E-Learning

Without close attention to building and maintaining functional communities of practice, even the most carefully designed online program can will degenerate as facilitators, support, and subject matter experts speak "at" each other instead of to or with each other. Granted, communities of practice in a distributed environment have a different look and feel than those that are forged in small groups in face-to-face settings. Nevertheless, they are vital if ongoing e-learning products and programs are to be developed, nurtured, and sustained. The main pillars of success -- communication, relevant tasks and outcomes, shared vision and mission, needs-responsive and ever-evolving instructional and developmental strategies -- will collapse.

What does a distributed community of practice look like in e-learning?

As in the case of typical communities of practice (CoP), the group members work together on many projects over time. They may not be on site together. However, they do communicate via e-mail, chat, project management interfaces, and collaboration tools.

Subject Matter Experts: Sometimes institutions use a subject matter expert to develop a single course. This is not always a good idea, particularly if one wishes to have an effective CoP develop over time. Ideally, a core of subject matter experts cooperate over time, and concern themselves with more content-integrative issues such as effective instructional strategy and emerging technologies.

Instructional Designers: Instructional designers are a vital part of the CoP. Their role can be a vexed one, however, if they do not have direct communication with the other members of the team, and do not adhere to a philosophy that encourages constant adaptation and modification to meet changing needs and challenges, they can be perceived as dictatorial, rigid, obstructive, out of date, or simply irrelevant.

Instructional Design Assistants: This is often the most overlooked piece in a CoP. It is important to have long-term, committed assistants who view their work as an apprenticeship and who are committed to keeping up-to-date with new versions of technologies as well as new and evolving approaches, such as video game-based simulation integrated into a conventional e-learning course.

Information Technology Team (includes Learning Object Coordinator): SCORM compliancy is more important vital than ever as learning objects must work across platforms and course management systems. Learning objects must be flexible enough to be shared in multiple applications, and a clear way of organizing access (files, server space, etc.) must be established at the outset and communicated clearly in order to avoid chaos, and to accommodate expansion in the future. Learning objects, properly classified and organized, should migrate easily with expansions and uploads. This may sound trivial, but anyone who has experienced a portal or system upgrade knows that it is not. All the course management system design, portal design, learning object development, etc. are for naught if the objects they employ are scattered randomly through different folders and on different servers.

Project Manager: The project manager should have a clear sense of the big picture as well as the details, and should be able to classify them into hierarchies. Project managers who cannot differentiate forest from trees are not helpful to their team, and will essentially drive a wedge in an emerging CoP. They should be able to guide the group by developing effective project management approaches that mesh with the culture of the organization. For example, a simple GANTT chart or Critical Path can help individuals set milestones and organize work.

Facilitators (Instructors): The instructors are often overlooked in the development of a Community of Practice. Although they should be required to participate in training and to be familiar with instructional Best Practices, as well as cognizant of effective instructional strategies, they are often kept on the periphery, and are marginalized, often for control issues. Their feedback is vital, however, particularly in terms of maintaining an evolutionary stance to instructional strategies, and reporting on the effectiveness of learning objects.

The following points can assist in creating distributed communities of practice for e-learning programs:

* Control of learning is distributed among the participants (e.g. students and instructors) and does not rest in the hands of a single subject matter expert or instructor.

* Learning activities are flexible, and modifications are encouraged if they suit the needs of the learner and the group as a whole.

*Multiple parties interact and they are united by a shared goal, problem or project, which provides a mission, vision, and focus. Incentives - both intrinsic and extrinsic - are incorporated into the learning environment in order to motivate learners.

*Learners and Facilitators are committed to the sharing of knowledge, and to encouraging the generation of new knowledge.

*Multiple perspectives and alternative explanations are not only encouraged, but required of learners and facilitators.

* Investigations and inquiries cross traditional disciplinary boundaries.

*Conceptual and intellectual risk-taking is encouraged and rewarded.

*Instructors should model intellectual risk-taking and innovative approaches to problem-solving.

*Instructional designers utilize appropriate instructional technology in order to actualize the development of a community of practice. In most instances, the activities will be structured around and within a course management system, which both foments and constricts the construction of a flexible learning space.

Nevertheless, the following strategies should be accommodated (Collins, 1991) and Nardi (1996):

Collaboration and Social Negotiation: Encourage the members to collaborate on projects. The project manager can facilitate this, and determine the most effective approach. Sometimes collaborative software is vital. At other times, simply using a blog can help encourage thinking and responding to ideas.

Exploration: A community of practice that does not encourage exploration -- both of curriculum (content) and new techniques (software and hardware) will quickly find that individuals will lose interest, and the e-learning courses will flounder. A word of caution, though -- one needs to be aware of who and what is driving change. If changes are made by the IT side of things without explaining the benefits to the others, or without getting their buy-in, large-scale failures are likely. Too-frequent change is as demotivating as no change at all.

Problem-Solving: Collaborative problem solving is perhaps one of the most immediate benefits of effective CoPs. Problem-solving can be technically focused, or can revolve around curriculum. For maximum effectiveness, however, it is vital to pay attention to marketing and outreach in order to maintain an awareness of the emerging and evolving needs of students.

Reflective Thinking: If a desired learning outcome includes the development of reflective thinking, then it is important that each member of the CoP contemplate how they can play a role in achieving the goal. For example, facilitators can think of ways to interact with learners to encourage reflective thinking. Instructional designers can think of activities. SMEs can bring new readings and content to bear. Instructional technologists can develop new applications of technologies -- simulations, etc.

The most effective instructional strategies analyze the desired objectives and then frame them in terms of the learning outcomes. Appropriate approaches keep the technology in the background, and foreground the cognitive processes at work.

References

C. van Winkelen. Inter-Organizational Communities of Practice. http://www.elearningeuropa.info/doc.php?id=1483&lng=1&doc lng=1

Resources from van Winkelen

1. Hubert, C., B. Newhouse, and W. Vestal, Building and Sustaining Communities of Practice. in Next-Generation Knowledge Management: Enabling Business Processes. 2001. Houston, USA.
2. van Winkelen, C. and P. Ramsell, Building Effective Communities. in Henley Knowledge Management Forum Second Annual Conference. 2002. Henley Management College.
3. Wenger, E. and W. Snyder, Communities of Practice: The Organizational Frontier. Harvard Business Review, 2000. 78(1): p. 139-145.
4. Gongla, P. and C. Rizzuto, Evolving Communities of Practice: IBM Global Services Experience. IBM Systems Journal, 2001. 40(4): p. 842-862.
5. Wenger, E., R. McDermott, and W. Snyder, Cultivating Communities of Practice. 2002: Harvard Business School Press.
6. Wenger, E., R. McDermott, and W.M. Snyder, Cultivating Communities of Practice. 2002, Boston, Mass: Harvard Business School Publishing.
7. Lawrence, T., N. Philips, and C. Hardy, Watching whale watching. Exploring the discursive foundations of collaborative relationships. Journal of Applied Behavioural Science, 1999. 35(4): p. 479-502.
8. Miles, R., C. Snow, and G. Miles, The Future.org. Long Range Planning, 2000. 33(3): p. 300-321.
9. Ashby, W.R., An Introduction to Cybernetics. 1956, London: Chapman and Hall.

10. Park, S.H. and G.T. Ungson, Interfirm rivalry and managerial complexity. Organization Science, 2001. 12(1): p. 37-53.
11. Johnson, G. and K. Scholes, Exploring Corporate Strategy. Sixth Edition. 2002, Harlow: Pearson Education Ltd.
12. Inkpen, A.C., Learning, knowledge acquisition and strategic alliances. European Management Journal, 1998. 16(2): p. 223-229.
13. LaPorte, B., Knowledge is currency at the World Bank. KM Review, 2002. 5(5): p. 10-13.
14. Skapinker, M., The Change Agenda. 2002, CIPD: London.
15. Boisot, M.H., Knowledge Assets; Securing Competitive Advantage in the Knowledge Economy. 1998, Oxford: Oxford University Press.
16. McKenzie, J. and C. van Winkelen, Understanding the Knowledgeable Organization: Nurturing Knowledge Competence. (Forthcoming). 2003, London: Thomson Learning.
17. Kwiecien, S. and D. Wolford, Gaining real value through best-practice replication. Knowledge Management Review, 2001. 4(1): p. 12-15.
18. Stewart, T.A., Intellectual Capital: The New Wealth of Organizations. 1997, New York: Doubleday.
19. van Winkelen, C. and P. Ramsell, Aligning value is key to designing communities. Knowledge Management Review, 2003. 5(6): p. 20-23.
20. Owens, D. and E. Thompson, Fusing learning and knowledge at the St. Paul Companies. Knowledge Management Review, 2001. 4(3): p. 24-29.
21. Braun, P., Digital knowledge networks: Linking communities of practice with innovation. Journal of Business Strategies, 2002. 19(1): p. 43-54.
22. Adler, P.S. and S.-W. Kwon, Social Capital; Prospects for a new concept. Academy of Management Review, 2002. 27(1): p. 17-40.
23. Lesser, E. and K. Everest, Using Communities of Practice to Manage Intellectual Capital. Ivey Business Journal, 2001. 65(4): p. 37-41.
24. Botkin, H. and C. Seeley, The Knowledge Management Manifesto: Why KM requires community-building. Knowledge Management Review, 2001. 3(6): p. 16-21.

25. Tosey, P., The peer learning community: a contextual design for learning? Management Decision, 1999. 37(5): p. 403-410.

Cross-Training and Cross-Tasking in Distance Program Development and Administration

Cross-training, a concept well understood in athletics and physical conditioning, is an excellent metaphor and model for an approach to build capacity and flexibility in online and distance education programs. Cross-training members of different teams (instructional, support services, academic resources, information technology, etc.) can lead to "cross-tasking," which is an approach that will allow for flexible, timely, and effective responses to changing needs, technology, content, and organizational structure.

The Goals of Cross-Training and Cross-Tasking:

As in physical condition, the goal of cross-training is not to become an expert in any one of the sports or activities one practices. Instead, by learning the fundamentals of the various physical activities or sports, one learns more about how the sport works, what one has to do to practice it successfully, and how and why the practitioners think the way they do, and what rationale underlies their decisions. Further, by learning the fundamentals of different sports with the goal of practicing them (even if at a rudimentary level), one increases one's own capacity to expand and grow. Flexibility -- in terms of both physical and mental agility -- is enhanced.

Cross-tasking takes the cross-trained team members and gives them an opportunity to put their skills to work in new applications.

Applying Cross-Training to Online and Distance Programs

If we apply the training metaphor, we could think of it as a person who cross-trains regularly in long-distance running, volleyball, swimming, gymnastics, pilates, and archery, who is suddenly asked to take up a new kind of aerobics class at the gym that involves elements of dance, gymnastics, pilates, and passing a ball back and forth. The new activity would take the person into unexplored territory, but the building blocks and conceptual underpinnings, plus the basic physical skills would be intact.

In terms of learning theory, we could say that the meta-cognitive resources would be in place. The behaviorist elements -- the skills, the physical actions, the connection between mind and body -- are familiar enough to be mastered. Finally, from a constructivist standpoint, the individual makes connections to lived experience, so that an experiential learning element comes into play, and the activity is situated within practice or even an apprenticeship mode. The combination of factors sets the stage for an individual who can quickly master the skills needed to accomplish desired outcomes, and better -- to think of creative solutions to problems and innovative ways to improve effectiveness and efficiency.

Cross-training for individuals in distance programs could involve the following items, but it is definitely not all-inclusive.

---*Software used by support services:* An understanding of the functions, capabilities, and limits of the software used for such services as registration, enrollment management, bursar (fiscal) issues, student records, etc. can help members of other teams fully utilize the functionality, as well as provide possible new applications and solutions to problems.

---*Software used in instruction:* A basic understanding of the various course management systems and learning platforms can yield significant benefits as individuals in other departments and units confront changing learner needs, platform and infrastructure changes, and the need to produce elements that interface with the management systems (whether commercially purchased or open-source). These include learning object repositories, digital library resources, shared and reusable course content, student and staff data.

---*Instructional design theory:* The lack of understanding of what makes a learning environment effective is one of the largest impediments to growth in any distance program. While it might be tempting to compartmentalize this function and leave it in the hands of instructional designers or course developers, it is vitally important for the institution that faculty, academic advisors, course facilitators and support, and academic unit staff be conversant in the rudiments of theory. In addition to being able to better advise students, individuals are able to grow as conditions and circumstances change.

---*Educational psychology:* Perhaps it is not necessary to go into great detail in all the various theories, but it is very good for all individuals who are involved in a distance program to be able to describe and utilize theories of motivation, learning acquisition, self-regulation / control of one's environment, self-concept, self-efficacy, collaborative learning, etc. Although the application is distance education, many of the theories apply to the workplace and workforce development.

---*Hardware and infrastructure:* Although very few members of the online or distance education enterprise will need to know details about the hardware and infrastructure configurations, an understanding of how they work and where limitations and opportunities occur is very important. Solutions to capacity issue are rarely as straightforward as simply implementing an in-house server farm. It is necessary to think of the entire enterprise, and develop policies, procedures, and new alliances that maintain the integrity of a program, allow for scalability, and assure security.

Cross-Tasking:

Cross-tasking means taking cross-training one step further, so that the cross-trained individuals are viewed as members of multiple teams, in addition to having a place in their core unit. This allows a greater responsiveness to new opportunities and it keeps people from getting "stuck" in one place, unit, or function. Further, it empowers the individual by providing skills that act as a kind of insurance policy against obsolescence or the slow decline of a unit or program. By finding growth and program opportunities in teaming and partnering, the temptation to "silo" opportunities and hoard information is lessened, and more efficient uses of resources are possible.

Benefits of Cross-Training and Cross-tasking:

---Enhanced problem-solving
---Team-building
---Eliminating silos and information hoarding
---Motivates employees to seek new opportunities and to be valued across the organization
---Encourages individuals to think in terms of the enterprise, and to suggest appropriate and productive partnering and consortia-building
---Solutions found for problems at unit level, rather than escalating
---Members able to envision new possibilities, make connections where they did not previously exist
---Units are more flexible and responsive to needs
---Units can work in flexible and ever-changing teams
---Increases team-member self efficacy and self concept, which is to say that they feel more confident, creative, and empowered, with an enhanced sense of self-worth and survivability in a rapidly changing work environment

Concrete Measurable Results of Cross-Training and Cross-Tasking:

---Quicker response time for student issues
---Lower turnover
---Higher employee productivity, measured in units produced and student success rates
---More efficient use of resources
---Institution-building new initiatives generated (new programs, new business ideas, which can build student base, enhance revenues or attract partners for new initiatives)

While there are many benefits to cross-training and cross-tasking, one would be remiss in not mentioning some of the risks. Very good management must be in place, and real commitment from the institution must support the endeavor. What is occurring is a shift in philosophy as well as function, and these can be very disruptive to an institution without a unifying message or vision that brings it together. Constant reward and reinforcement of positive achievements must occur and team members need to be constantly reassured that their efforts are enhancing their long-term viability and value to the organization.

Cross-training and cross-tasking are most effective in times of rapid change -- particularly when the changes are externally driven and include technology, institutional, and economic shifts. Because change comes accompanied with anxiety and chaos, the organization's leadership must be stable, focused and committed to managing change, and renewing one's commitment to a mission and vision where employees are acknowledged, listened to, and respected. If this is not in place, cross-training and cross-tasking will not achieve its full potential.

Please Make Me Think!

Creating Engaging and Relevant Online Courses

FIRST VODKA, NOW MADONNA: CHE GUEVARA IMAGE STILL SELLS

or

Using Pop Culture Images to Teach Students to Relocate the Dislocated Referent

Helping students become more aware of how images shape meaning is one of the primary objectives of media and popular culture courses. Online courses provide excellent opportunities to help students begin to understand how images create meaning. Such knowledge can empower students and help them learn to use images in conjunction with their own work.

An example drawn from popular culture is Madonna's 2003 release, *American Life.*

****

I'm just living out the American dream

And I just realised that nothing

Is what it seems

> ---- from Madonna's *American Life*

Most people watching Madonna's music and video offering, *American Life*, which debuted in April 2003 on the Internet at yahoo.com, launch.com, mp3.com, and other sites, probably did not recognize the visual allusions she makes in her beret, dark hair, severe expression, single red stars, military stencil distressed type font.

Madonna *American Life* (2003)

Others surely saw echoes of Alberto Korda's famous 1960 photo in which Argentina-born Marxist revolutionary Che Guevara, attending a funeral in Havana, wears a black beret emblazoned with a red star. Korda later complained when the famous image was used in 2000 in a Smirnoff ad to promote vodka sales. Korda, who supported the use of the image to promote such causes as the revolutionary overthrow of elitist governments or repressive regimes, vigorously opposed the use of the image to promote vodka.

Korda's photo of Che Guevara
based on Korda's Che photo

The Smirnoff ad

Very astute (and probably older) web-surfers probably noticed Madonna's image bears a striking resemblance to that of "Tania," the *nom du guerre* of Haydee Tamara Bunke Bider, who died in a 1967 ambush in Bolivia at age 29. Her remains were found in 1998 within a mile of those of Che Guevara. In the most famous photographs of Tania, she is wearing the same type of beret as Che Guevara.

"Tania" – Haydee Tamara Bunke Bider

Oddly, her photograph resonates with images of a beret-wearing Faye Dunaway as Bonnie in *Bonnie and Clyde,* which was released the same year as Tania's death, 1967.

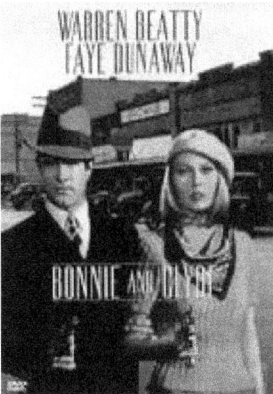

Bonnie and Clyde (1967)

Later, the "Tania" image was echoed in the 1974 images of the Symbionese Liberation Army (SLA) in which the newspaper heiress Patty Hearst, was reborn as, "Tania" an automatic weapon-wielding, beret-wearing bank robber and revolutionary. Although members of the group were implicated in murders, kidnappings, hostage-taking, and bank-robbery, they were serious anti-heroes in some circles, primarily those comprised of individuals who opposed the war in Vietnam.

"Tania" – Patty Hearst – 1974

In these cases, one can make the case that the use of the "Che" beret suggests affiliation with the revolutionary causes that Che Guevara fought for. The beret is effectively turned into a symbol, or a referent denoting "revolutionary" or "rebel." When the beret is positioned on the original "Tania" (Haydee) or the Patty Hearst "Tania," the referent is "relocated." In relocation, it exercises an iconographic function, and essentially "brands" the bearer.

With Madonna, the beret functions in similar ways. However, given the motives of the artist and the marketing machine behind the publicity, it becomes clear that the beret is a co-opted symbol, a referent "dislocated." The beret becomes a posturing, or, as Madonna might have put it a decade earlier, a "voguing" of a previous icon. Madonna's self-invention generally self-referential, and an obviously intentional act. *American Life,* however, purports to be more of a contemplation, almost a memoir.

It is not Madonna's first pass at co-opting a "text" that had, in its original version, a subversive message. Her use of the Che image strangely echoes her "remaking" of Lena Wertmuller's classic film, *Swept Away.* Wertmuller's original was a potent Marxist critique of elitism, classism, and oppression. In Madonna's hands, the intellectual content eliminated, and it becomes more of a pseudo-violent cartoon of Shakespeare's The Taming of the Shrew. Troublingly, Madonna's *Swept Away* legitimizes and/or attempts to eroticize violence toward women. It's familiar territory for Madonna, who has borrowed heavily from the gay underground, including the "rough trade" and sado-masochism scene. However, in the original there are true questionings of society, culture, and human nature. Madonna consistently presents a significantly mainstreamed version, palatable to consumers unaware of its provenance.

The beret helps Madonna package a product that promises to be an investigation of culture, gender roles, societal attitudes, cowboys, dance, fashion, and war. However, as the referent, the beret, is dislocated in the service of commerce and pop culture, it becomes not a symbol of affiliation with a revolutionary cause. Instead, it becomes a symbol of commercially-motivated metamorphosis and self-invention. *American Life* illustrates the process of packaging oneself and one's image. It also reflects the intentionality of manipulating graphics to show individuals in the process of creating and/or deliberately creating an identity, attempting to control the act of self-invention.

Miracle Herbal Cures from the Rain Forest: Purple Lapacho -- Anti-Cancer or Rain Forest Mirage?

This assignment gives you an opportunity to examine the arguments of writers, their use of logic, and the nature of the "evidence" they are using to support their claims. It also gives you a chance to look at two sides of the story, and to examine evidence through lenses colored by presuppositions, assumptions, beliefs, and values.

Can you think of highly touted product that has been promoted as a miracle cure? Do you believe all the claims? Some of the claims? Why? Why not?

Here is an example that will help you hone your critical thinking skills and your ability to evaluate information and sources. You may write your paper on the bark of the lapacho tree, or on any other item that has been hyped. (Vioxx? Certain diets? Vitamin E? Rock and crystal healing? Stem cells for curing Parkinson's?)

Does the bark of the lapacho tree (pau d'arco) cure cancer? Is this product the Amazon rain forest's natural Viagra? The lapacho tree, which is native to Paraguay, Brazil, and northern Argentina, is known for its gorgeous flowers. The descendants of the Guaranis, the indigenous peoples of the Alto Parana area, claim the inner bark has curative powers. Recently, lapacho bark has been tested as a cure for cancer, as well as a "vitality enhancing" elixir and potent aphrodisiac.

Whether lapacho contains active ingredients capable of bringing about the health benefits is a critical question, and a portal to a deeper issue. Do herbal remedies work? Are there "secrets of the shamans" that could be used for the good of humanity? If so, what are they? How do we test them? Some believe herbal remedies are more effective than conventional medicines, and are more affordable and accessible. Others believe that it herbal remedies are nothing more than snake oil. At best, they're not harmful. At worst, they could actually destroy one's health.

The Vivid Vision (Paragraph 1): A scene that depicts an array of herbal medicines (perhaps a scene from a health food store), perhaps an individual taking an herbal remedy.

Background and Definitions (Paragraph 2): What is the lapacho tree? Where is it found? Why is it considered medicinal? What part? Who used it? When? Why? *The key is to brainstorm with appropriate questions, to help bring into focus the topic.*

Who says so? Why? (Paragraph 3): This is a series of questions that are made to test the assumptions, beliefs, prejudices, and possible motives of the individuals who are saying things about the product.

What have people experienced? Testimonials. (Paragraphs 4 and 5). Are testimonials believable? Are they always legitimate? Find two or more and analyze them. Look for flaws in their arguments, or incomplete information.

What do you think? (Paragraph 6). Would you give lapacho bark a try? When? Where? Why? What do you think? What did you base your decision on? Please provide examples or personal testimonials.

Conclusion (Paragraph 7). Not completely necessary, if it has been covered earlier.

Useful Web Resources

Rain Forest Information: http://www.rain-tree.com/

Clinical Trials for Lapacho (Pau d'Arco) http://www.rain-tree.com/clinic/clinicp.htm#PAU

Sloan-Kettering Cancer Center: Lapacho
http://www.mskcc.org/mskcc/html/11571.cfm?recordid=399

Purple Lapacho: Ancient Herb, Modern Miracle?
http://www.oralchelation.com/taheebo/lapacho1.htm

Drug Digest: Lapacho.
http://www.drugdigest.org/DD/DVH/HerbsWho/0,3923,552793
%7CLapacho,00.html

What Is Lapacho Used For Today?
http://www.womenandinfants.com/body.cfm?id=388&chunkiid
=21797

Pau d'arco http://www.genhealth.com/pau_darco.htm

About Lapacho
http://www.cantron.com/html/nutraceuticals/lapacho.html

Questions About Herbal Remedies

Quackwatch: Your Guide to Quackery, Health Fraud, and
Intelligent Decisions. http://www.quackwatch.org/

Lies and Deceipt in Alternative Medicine:
http://www.valleyskeptic.com/altmed.htm

For that Health Glow, Drink Radiation! *Popular Science.*
http://www.popsci.com/popsci/science/bbdb0b4511b84010vgnv
cm1000004eecbccdrcrd.html

Heavy Metals in Ayurvedic Herbal Medicines. *ScienceWeek.*
http://scienceweek.com/2005/sc050204-6.htm

Snake Oil -- The Wikipedia Entry.
http://en.wikipedia.org/wiki/Snake_oil

Shipwrecks, Lost Gold, Pirate's Treasure Chests: The Process Essay

After Hurricanes Katrina, Rita, and Wilma, a number of people who had devoted their lives to searching for sunken pirate ships and buried treasure became very excited. The storms churned up the seas, eroded barrier islands, and uncovered vast expanses of ocean floor that had previously been covered with vegetation or debris. The enormous erosional event had fabulous implications. What did the storms uncover? Were chests of doubloons and sunken Spanish ships filled with gold coins, jewels, and other valuables now accessible? If so, how would one start to take advantage of it?

What is the process of putting together a treasure hunt?

This essay assignment gives an individual the opportunity to learn how to describe and write about a process. The process could even lead to a successful treasure hunt!

By examining the processes of groups who have been success, the writer can gain an appreciation of the necessary steps. For example, the Odyssey Marine Exploration group found and recovered a Civil War-era ship that sank during a storm in 1865. Located off the coast of Georgia, the ship was located in 1,700 feet of water. The Company recovered $75 million in gold and silver coins, as well as more than 13,000 artifacts.

The discovery was the culmination of a 10-year search by John Morris and Greg Stemm. The quest for was described in _Lost Gold of the Republic_ and in numerous websites, including the *National Geographic.* The divers recovered money from the Civil War. They had expected coins, gold, silver, treasure, pearls, artifacts, antiquities, hand-blown glass.

This is an excellent assignment which gives individuals an opportunity to learn how to analyze a process, as well as to connect it to an attractive goal.

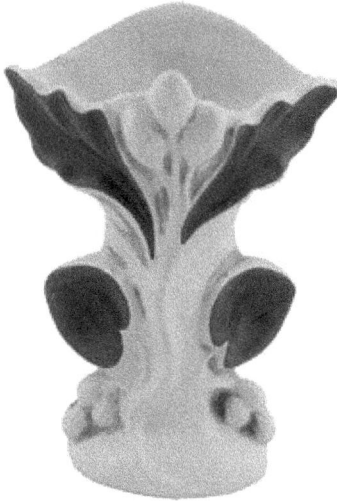

Artifact Replica from the SS Republic

In Action (Paragraph 1): A scene that depicts the storm that caused the shipwreck, and a glimpse of the treasure inside.

Desired Outcome -- Treasure! (Paragraph 2): In this paragraph, describe the type of treasure, the place, the reasons for it being where it is, the ship, the storm, the history and contexts. Then describe the desired outcome.

Who has found huge troves of treaure? Where? How? (Paragraph 3): Describe how one treasure-hunter found a shipwreck full of treasure.

How would you get started? Where do you begin? (Paragraphs 4 and 5). How did Odyssey explorationists know that there would be a shipwreck? Was there a legend? Was it believable? Where did they get their facts? How?

What would you do? If you had to put together a treasure exploration, where would you go?(Paragraph 6). Describe where, how, and why you would choose the place. Describe the process. Then, make a list of the equipment you would need, and the team. Are there any ethical issues? What would you do with any finds?

Conclusion (Paragraph 7). How much will it cost? How do you raise the money? Would this be worth exploring? Describe your conclusion.

Coins, gold, silver, treasure, pearls, artifacts, antiquities, hand-blown glass.

Useful Web Resources

Tag Cloud: Typical treasure in shipwrecks, Gold flowerettes, gold chains, bullion, ingots, silver, platinum, pearls, gold filigree, embossed metal boxes, mother of pearl, gold plated pistols, Mayan and Incan gold funerary items, wine bottles, goblets, crystal champagne flutes, gold stocks.

Odyssey Marine Exploration. *How do they do it?*: http://www.shipwreck.net/

Deep Dark Secrets: Shipwreck Hunters Find Benjamin Noble. (Lake Superior. http://www.cdnn.info/news/article/a041220.html

Shipwreck Salvage: Treasure Hunters vs. Archaeologists. http://ancienthistory.about.com/library/weekly/aa102098.htm

Deep Shipwreck Explorer's Association. http://ancienthistory.about.com/gi/dynamic/offsite.htm?site=http ://www.shipwreck.net/gpstemm/DEEPSEA.html

Mel Fisher's Treasure Site. http://www.melfisher.com/

The Ghost Galleon and the Santa Margarita shipwreck, and later treasure find. http://www.melfisher.com/salvage/go/atocha.asp

Pit Bull Brainstorming: The Great Concatenation of Questions

Brainstorming is an invention strategy for composition that can take many forms. While some find it useful to use diagrams, outlines, decision trees, and clusters, those tactics tend to focus on the "what" instead of the "how" and the "why." In order to approach deeper issues, and to trigger chains of thoughts, a very powerful technique is to develop series of questions. The brainstorming revolves around questions that trigger questions.

It is a chain of questions, or, one could say a "great concatenation of questions." This approach is extremely useful for causal essays, as well as basic argumentation. One topic that certainly helps illustrate the technique is that of the American Pit Bull Terrier. It seems that attacks by pit bulls just keep increasing. Why is it happening? What are we doing about it? Are some dog breeds being labeled "bad breeds"?

Audio: I listened to an interesting report on National Public Radio entitled, "Targeting Aggressive Dog Breeds in California." I accessed it through the National Public Radio website located here:
http://www.npr.org/templates/story/story.php?storyId=5012365

I was able to listen to the show using Real Player, which I had downloaded for free from the Internet. Alternatively, I could have listened to it using Windows Media Player.

Questions immediately came to mind. I thought about the general questions, and I found my questions were helping me narrow my topic.

The perplexing questions first:
Why do pit pulls attack people, and how can such a tiny dog be so dangerous?
Who says they're bad? Why are they saying it?
What do some people want to do? Where? Why?

History and background thoughts:
Why are pit bulls aggressive? Were they bred that way?
What is a pit bull, and what makes it so dangerous?
Who uses the ultra-aggressive pit bulls?
Who might need such an aggressive dog?

The other side of the coin:
What is good about a pit bull?
Why do some people say the breed is very loving?
Can pit bulls be friendly, happy dogs?

Let's get personal:
What would I do if I had a pit bull?
Training, conditioning, behavior modification
Are there any business opportunities here? Yes! one can
specialize in deprogramming dangerous dogs; also, let your city
become the pit bull dumping ground next to a major
metropolitan area (all dogs must be muzzled, though)
Dog chow for ultra aggressive dogs (make them more
aggressive) -- is there and ethical issue here?
Pacifying dog chow (calm down and tranquilize the dogs)

Tag Cloud: pit bull terriers, composition strategies,
brainstorming techniques, concept mapping, clusters of
thoughts, invention techniques, first year composition, mad dog,
mauling dogs, 76-year-old-woman mauled by pit bull as
grandchildren watch in horror, Denver bans pit bulls, Nederland,

Colorado becomes aggressive breed haven, new kennel accepts cast-off killer canines

Useful Websites for Information

Pit Bull Primer: There are two sides to the pit bull banning debate
San Francisco Chronicle, October 30, 2005
http://www.sfgate.com/cgi-bin/article.cgi?f=/c/a/2005/10/30/CMGTAF0PGA1.DTL

Pit Bull Attack Places Breed Ban in the Spotlight
Suburban Chicago News, November 20, 2005
http://www.suburbanchicagonews.com/couriernews/top/3_1_EL20_A1PITBULL_S1.htm

Pit Bull Apologists, Wake Up. San Francisco Chronicle, July 6, 2004. http://sfgate.com/cgi-bin/article.cgi?f=/c/a/2004/07/06/BAG0C7H3811.DTL

Elmhurst Woman Mauled by Pit Bull, New York Daily News, November 23, 2005.
http://nydailynews.com/front/story/368399p-313288c.html

Piracy in the Straits of Malacca: An Interactive Exercise

Imagine being issued a handheld computer, an mp3 player, a CD-ROM, and then being told that you will have to develop a plan to deal with the problem of piracy and attacks on ships in the Straits of Malacca. You will work with a team of 10 classmates who will be constantly traveling, and who will have only intermittent access to the Internet. You will be expected to develop components of a plan that you can implement together when you meet again, either face to face, or through synchronous Internet communication.

Mission (Outcome) Centered E-Learning Experience

You must, with your teammates, devise a plan to deal with piracy in the Straits of Malacca. You have certain equipment and funds available at your disposal. You have a certain amount of political clout, and you have some indirect methods that you can use.

While it is still possible to work as a team even while separated, the mission must be further refined, and broken into steps that can be implemented.

After refining the mission, and breaking it down into action steps, the areas of action should be mapped out. This must be done after understanding the nature of the problem.

Partial expanded definition of the problem:

- Cargo ships are attacked when they reach the "pinch point" through the Straits of Malacca.
- Ships are commandeered and their cargo sold on the black market.
- Crew are often killed, but sometimes kidnapped.
- The crews that do the pirating are not the same people as the individuals who fund the activities.

- Economic pressures, political double-dealing, poverty, and corruption make piracy appealing.
- Sovereignty issues come into play when policing and monitoring activities are proposed. Who would monitor traffic and police it? How is integrity assured?
- Logistics are challenging. GPS monitoring, identification of ships, cargo, monitoring of cargo, safety issues, are complicating factors.
- Trafficking and poor reporting of cargo also complicate the issue. Possible problem areas: human smuggling, illegal substances, contraband, falsified merchandise (pharmaceuticals, licensed brand "knock offs," counterfeit equipment and spare parts, etc.).

Team roles and responsibilities:

Students must distribute roles and assume responsibility for developing their piece of the plan in anticipation of when they get together.

The roles can be those of advisors.

- Physical Security advisor
- Geopolitical Affairs advisor
- Natural Resources advisor
- Trade and Trafficking advisor
- Maritime navigation advisor

Each must come up with a plan, which can follow a very prescribed approach. The responses can be shaped around a template or guiding questions.

Because not everyone will have the same sort of access to information, each person should collect information for distribution in the following forms:

- Text files (Word)
- mp3 Audio files for uploading and downloading to portable players

- Graphics -- maps, interactive mileage calculators, navigation maps, charts with statistics, navigation charts and calculators, examples of contraband and counterfeits, movies

Distributed Learning Space (Network-Centric)

By realizing that one is separated by time zones, access, and space from one's teammates, the team must come up with ways to communicate. Step 1 involves finding out the best way for everyone to communicate. It may be that everyone is on the same sort of network and can communicate via handheld (BlackBerry, Treo, T-Mobile Sidekick), either through text messages, voice, or instant message. It may be that some of the team members will be out of range, or, due to security reasons, will not have an interactive system.

In that case, there must be a way for them to role-play without frequent communication, and to make the times when sending information is possible really count. Whatever the communication constraints, a solution to being in touch and accomplishing the goal must be devised.

Step 2 involves developing a procedure for distributing the information needed by team members at the appropriate time. Some information will need to be made available "on demand." The Advisor's reports need to be shared in a way that works for everyone.

Distributed Leadership (Network-Centric)

Instruction to students: Please read the articles and devise your own plan to deal with piracy in the Straits of Malacca. Keep in mind that the Straits of Malacca pose regional security, socio-economic, political, and strategic problems.

Pedagogical / Implementation realities: The students will be working individually, but yet, as they do so, they will be envisioning how their piece of the puzzle fits with the others.

They will be taking full responsibility for their role as an Advisor, and they realize that they must do a good job when they meet with the other Advisors so that they can work together to achieve the goal of creating a plan.

Some Advisors will find that the information provided to all is sufficient. Others will not. Thus, they need to be able to get information on an as-needed basis.

Because not everyone will have the luxury of a lot of storage space, or access to the Internet, it is useful to have all the readings and information available on the web, in easy-to-download files.

An audio version should also be available, ideally as an mp3 in an audio file. Later, the Advisor can listen through a handheld computer or through an iPod portable player. Graphics and other learning objects should be optimized for display in many different players, and delivery modes.

The Initial Readings for the Advisors.

Maritime terrorists lurk in S-E Asia : -- http://beyondutopia.net/creative-problem/malacca-straits/malacca-1.htm

The Straits of Malacca and the waters off Indonesia are becoming hotspots for pirates -- http://beyondutopia.net/creative-problem/malacca-straits/malacca-2.htm

Navy looking for sailors abducted in the Straits of Malacca -- http://beyondutopia.net/creative-problem/malacca-straits/malacca-3.htm

Malacca Straits remains one of most dangerous shipping lanes in world -- http://beyondutopia.net/creative-problem/malacca-straits/malacca-4.htm

Straits of Malacca: Security Implications (map) --
http://www.saag.org/papers11/paper1033.html

Advisors Strategy Meeting.

The final step in the course is to plan an Advisors' Strategy Meeting. This is when the final plan is developed. This is, in essence, a final project. However, with the "extreme situatedness" of the assignment, it is possible that some of the plan could be further studied by interested parties and actually implemented.

Taking a Class on Shakespeare on T-Mobile SideKick or Cell Phone -- A Few Ideas

New flexible technologies make teaching and learning Shakespeare a raw, exciting, and relevant event. Envision a course called Love, Madness, and Shakespeare. It is possible using embedded journalist and video game-inspired collaborative strategies with the blend of portable devices, wireless laptops, desktop computers with high-speed or dial-up modem Internet access, and/or face-to-face instruction to accommodate your students' needs and situations.

Why would you want to do this? It sounds like a lot of work, doesn't it. Well, the rewards are most definitely worth it. Just check it out. Done well, studying Shakespeare can be a heart-pounding limit experience where you find out about yourself and the psychology of larger-than-life characters. It's emotionally intimate. The thrill is so intense it almost feels "wrong" - toying with the taboo, exposure, violence, longing, death.

Why doesn't someone make a video game of this stuff??

Why not, indeed?

Imagine in *Romeo and Juliet,* being able to role-play the various characters. After watching clips from Baz Luhrmann's *Romeo+Juliet* to get an idea about how one director envisioned updating the classic play, one can get an idea of how to make the experience intense, immediate, and personal for the student.

You can ask students to design a video game – or, at least break up the components of the video-gaming experience and create activities for web-based course instruction.

Music. Before *Romeo+Juliet,* Baz Luhrmann was well-known for directing music videos. The soundtrack for the film takes emotional orchestration to a new level. It is, in many ways, like the various forms of electronic music – trance, chill-out music, etc. – which is purposefully designed to manage moods. Ask a student to create a soundtrack for a scene that they will rewrite, inserting themselves. They can select music clips they've downloaded and create a list, or mix a CD. Then they can write themselves into a scene, modifying it to fit their own lives, and the current world. These can be posted and shared.

Personal Mask-Making and Identity Shifting. Part of the intensity of *Romeo and Juliet* involves exploring the hidden knowledge you encounter when you wear a mask. In a video game, you would need to be able to disguise yourself. Actually, you can disguise not only yourself, but death itself. Think of the sleeping potion that made one mimic death. Think of the scene in the crypt – being the only one alive – life masked as death, and under a house of death, one finds life. Ask students to design masks for the costume party. How would they design them? Ask them to use symbols, visual metaphors, etc. in their masks, then post them on the Internet (or in a folder / blog) for others to see & comment on.

Verona.com – Embedded Journalism in Walled Cities, Plague, Death, and Death's Antidotes. We enter the madness of civilization in all of Shakespeare's plays. The dynamics we find in Shakespeare reinvent themselves – ethnic clashes, mafias and rival gangs, plague, quarantine, and the contemplation of death's antidotes. The sense of danger, creeping paranoia, and a repressive social system are elevated to an intense degree in *Romeo and Juliet.*

Students can become "embedded reporters" in Shakespeare's world – and in their role as investigative journalists and news editors, they can create their own newspaper based on the play. Ask students to view theonion.com, nytimes.com, and sfgate.com.

Then ask students to create their own news website. Ask them to describe how and why they chose their headlines, the graphics, the captions, and the arrangement on the page. You may wish to provide a template, either in Word or in a web-editing program such as Dreamweaver or a free one downloadable from the Internet. They can also do a "Verona Radio" as podcasts. Ask them to explain how and why they chose the stories, the background sounds, and the music.

Romeo's Reality Television: A twist on reality television can be made here. Can students imagine "Survivor" reconfigured to incorporate the elements of *Romeo and Juliet?* Could they for "Idol" or any other kind of reality television show? Ask them to think about it, explain it, explore it.

This "Romeo" Life: A popular public radio show, "This American Life," could be recast to be "This Romeo and Juliet Life," or, simply, "This Romeo Life," with the structure of autobiographical experience, cultural commentary, and psychological insight found in "This American Life."

These are just a few ideas to get started. The idea is to make Shakespeare an immersion experience that emphasizes the human emotions that animate the dramas.
Love, madness, and Shakespeare. First the course, now the experience!!

The "Bambi Effect" -- Why We Hate It When Cute Creatures (or Beliefs) Are Threatened or Harmed

Students in online courses are often offended by comments in a discussion forum or by blog postings. Evolution, Disney characters, fascist propaganda techniques, advertising's depictions of ideal beauty, "pop" sensationalists and taboos (Michael Jackson, Janet Jackson, Madonna), modernist art installations (even *Christo's Gates* in New York City in January-February 2005) arouse emotional attacks instead of open-mindedness. Often accused of excessive "political correctness," instructors find themselves powerless to stop the knee-jerk reactions.

One step is to ask students to ask themselves whether or not they find themselves mystified or annoyed by the observations and analyses of texts and popular culture? The following text can be of great help in understanding the approach that is taken in much literary and cultural criticism.

The World Is a Text: Writing, Reading, and Thinking About Culture and Its Context.

By Jonathan Silverman and Dean Rader. Upper Saddle River, NJ: Prentice-Hall, 2003.

Although *The World Is a Text* was designed as a reader to accompany first-year college composition classes, it is an invaluable source of readings and interpretive strategies. Not only does it open one's eyes to the multiplicity of interpretive possibilities embodied in all "texts" (literary, cultural, phenomenological), it also helps one understand how scholars can say the things they do about video-game based movies such as *Tomb Raider*, nutritional supplement advertising, the design of theme parks, political campaign television "spots."

An introduction to semiotics, deconstructive philosophy, rhetoric, post-colonial discourse, gender studies, and post-structural thought, the text teaches students how to "read" and find meaning in "texts" of all sorts. Texts are more than the printed word. They are any decodable thing, and it is assumed that they possess the capacity to either generate or mediate meaning.

How we, as readers, make meaning is something we often take for granted until we take a look at how we have been conditioned by society, experience, and convention to attach certain meanings to certain symbols. The fact that this process is often unconscious makes us all the more malleable and subject to manipulation. A good example is what sportsmen and conservationists call "The Bambi Effect," which, briefly stated, explains the revulsion we feel when cute woodland creatures are harmed or threatened.

A. Waller Hastings' article in *The Journal of Popular Film and Television* describes how identification, anthropomorphism, and transfer occur by means of semiotics and film narrative. Savage Art Resources further explores and comments on the phenomenon with an installation in their gallery consisting of the work of ten artists. Named *The Bambi Effect,* the pieces of art include Robyn O'Neil's drawing "It Produces Food and He Taketh Away," a visual commentary on the intrusiveness of modern, synthetic-clothed man in the environment. The bottom line is this: be aware of when you are being manipulated. Do not accept everything at face value. Emotions are powerful persuasive tools, particularly when unleashed by images that evoke nationalistic fervor, family bonds, the idea of innocence assaulted, etc.

Leni Riefenstahl understood the power of images to evoke a sense of national identity, individual, and collective power. She became known (and reviled) as Hitler's favorite filmmaker, and architect of masterful propaganda films. In fact, her film version of Hitler's 1934 Nuremberg rally, *Triumph of the Will,* has been considered one of the best propaganda films ever made. When she died at age 101, the commentary on her work, vision, and context, *The Wonderful, Horrible Life of Leni Riefenstahl,* received renewed attention. It does seem a bit strange that two of the Nazi Party's most effective propagandists and apologists were women: first, in the form of <u>Elizabeth Forster-Nietzsche</u> (Friedrich's sister), who helped construct a "philosophy" for the party through her careful editing of her brother's work; and second, in the form of a visual artist, Leni Riefenstahl.

Once we become aware of how and why we believe what we believe, and once we become conscious of how we interpret our perceptions, we can start to question each cognitive step along the meaning-making road.

Along the way, we must accept that there are multiple interpretations for each set of signs, and that texts (as repositories of signs) can have multiple meanings.

The interpretive strategies that are employed can be profoundly destabilizing, even emotionally troubling to readers. What do you do when it is suggested that "truth" and "reality" are constructs?

Further, many readers are upset by the notion that politics, persuasion, and power manifest themselves in *all* texts at the moment in which an individual seeks to assign or make meaning from them.

There is nothing to fear – the fact that there are different ways to read and interpret texts is a robust endeavor, dating back as far as Augustine's *City of God,* Books XX and XXII, where he discusses how one passage of scripture can have literal, moral, allegorical, and anagogical meanings.

Nevertheless, the experience of interpreting texts -- in whatever form they occur -- images, mp3s, film -- and in whatever delivery method one uses, makes the ability to engage in robust discursive analysis more important than ever.

Courses that Encourage Diversity

When one enters the relatively bland learning space of an online or hybrid distance course, it is very tempting to think that the learners will be as uniform and predictable as the interface itself. If each course has the "same look and feel," does the blandness precondition the learner to think that all the other learners will similarly possess the "same look and feel" as all the other e-learners? How will the e-learner consider other learners in the course with him or her? Will they be assumed to be all the same, too? Will the learner be unconsciously conditioned to assume that all the learners are mere echoes (or mirror images) of himself or herself?

Uniformity has its virtues, but I think we need to think twice before we jump in and semiotically engineer the e-learning space to have a mass-produced, bland, predictable appearance.

I understand the arguments for uniformity of design. In fact, I've been a proponent of it. My arguments have revolved around the quest for navigability and a desire to do whatever possible to increase learner self-efficacy, which translates to self-confidence, more time on task, enhanced motivation, and higher completion rates.

However, I think I've been overlooking a critical point. If the design is too uniform, does it tacitly discourage contemplating a reality that deviates from the cookie-cutter norm? Even if it is easy to navigate, does the design inhibit the expression of multiple points of view because each person is constrained by the rigidities of the discussion board?

Further, in the rush to mass-produce courses in a centralized (or outsourced) e-learning factory, are we running the risk of eliminating the possibility of creative innovation? In the rush to be standard, are we demotivating learners by failing to capture their attention? Do we fail to provide stimulation, thus making it more "work?" What happens when the learner starts to expect to have to slog through the course material and activities?

Boredom is one thing. Exclusion is another. One of the great promises of distance distributed education is its potential to bring together individuals from diverse backgrounds, locations, socio-economic conditions, jobs, family structures, and geopolitical contexts. In theory, one can learn strategies in the e-learning space that could apply to society at large, in terms of uniting individuals via a common mission.

Conflict resolution, creative problem-solving, mediation, leadership, and organizational behavior are just a few of the activities that can (and should) be practiced in the diversity-inflected e-learning space.

Unfortunately, this is not likely to happen in the learning space, where discussion threads are indistinguishable from each other, and learners tend to parrot the same things, or try to anticipate what they think the instructor wants to read.

Deeper learning is less likely as well, as students tend to focus on "skill and drill" activities to prepare themselves for timed quizzes. Situated learning activities, with interesting and relevant questions are difficult to mass produce. A cookie cutter course starts looking like the digital equivalent of a textbook. This is fine to a point. The content has been reviewed for accuracy and relevancy, and learning objectives have been clearly stated. However, the dynamic aspects of learning are absent.

Encourage diverse identity-development. Anthropologists have long questioned the idea that any culture is capable of developing a "type section," or archetypal example of it, in its "essential" form. Instead, they suggest that cultural identity is *always* in flux, and that it and the individuals who comprise it, are constantly adjusting themselves, and adapting themselves to social situations. The e-learning space, if flexible enough, gives individuals a perfect opportunity to "morph" as much as they wish, and to exchange ideas, debate, incorporate, and create their own learning artifacts.

Practice "vision-building" by means of collectively thinking of multiple ways to achieve learning objectives. In stating a learning objective, or desired outcome, one has essentially set out a mission and a vision statement. The e-learning space gives the facilitator the opportunity to guide the learners individually and collectively toward a common goal.

Encourage learners to upload and share work. If there is a way for students to access short papers and/or projects, it can be quite helpful to others. Not only does it help individuals share techniques and thus become more adept at using software and analytical tools, it provides support for brainstorming and making connections.

Connect activities to the real world, then ask students to share with each other. Even though learners may be in different parts of the world and may seem to have little in common, it is possible to find points of discussion and to share perspectives. For example, in a class, "Leadership in Difficult Times," learners studied post-traumatic stress syndrome, and then were given the opportunity to share experiences and insights. Although the learners were scattered around the globe, and consisted of military personnel and civilians, they found common ground in this area and shared meaningful ideas that immediately benefited the participants, many of whom were wrestling with leadership and personal dilemmas having to do with traumatic incident stress.

Ask students to discuss items that have multiple points of view or perspectives. Sometimes more light-hearted assignments and activities yield the most results. The students have a chance to share their personal approaches, experience, likes, and dislikes. An example is to write and share reviews of movies, music, or books. They can also share opinions of news items and current events, from multiple perspectives. This encourages flexible thinking, and making connections.

Discuss ethical dilemmas. Rather than asking students to simply "take sides," ask them to look at various points within an ethical dilemma, and to discuss potential impact of possible decisions. This can also lead to productive role-playing and simulation.

Require blogs. Encourage students to link to personal blogs. The blogs can be multi-faceted -- they can be a space to present a project in a virtual presentation, and they can also allow students to upload graphics, photos, music, audio, and video to promote diversity -- not only of ideas, but also of presentation and image.

Encourage podcasting. Ask students to record brief audio clips (with a written transcript), to share the sound of their voices. This will provide more depth, and prompt different forms of creativity.

Consider incorporating avatars. Some people may say that this is not "serious" and it detracts from learning. However, it is quite possible that just the opposite is the case, particularly when one takes a look at the interfaces of the major instant messaging providers: Yahoo, AOL Instant Messenger, MSN, etc. In fact, one of the most aggressive early instant messaging providers, ICQ, became instantly recognizable through their little "daisy" motif, and the wide range of avatars that were made available to users.

Make the discussion space more lively. Use color, signs, avatars. This is an excellent opportunity to learn from video games and simulations. If players (users) have an opportunity to personalize their self-presentation, and to communicate messages in non-verbal ways, it opens up a new level of sharing of ideas, and appreciation of diversity. Encourage role-playing and simulation, and ask people to develop an appreciation for a point of view they had previously not considered.

There are many other ways that the design of a course, as well as the instructional strategies can encourage diversity. Ironically, perhaps the most used model of course development and design is also one of the surest ways to discourage thinking in terms of diversity and inclusion. Further, the "cookie cutter course" demotivates the learner.

The same can be said for learning objects, and learning object repositories, if the focus strays from learning outcomes, and becomes fixated on efficient production of courses. One might be tempted to argue that diversity in an online course is simply not relevant -- that uniformity and standardization are absolutely necessary given the need to pass standardized tests.

Interestingly, this argument falls apart under the pressure of tests. In order to perform well, students must be able to synthesize information and apply it in a number of ways. In order to get to that point, the learner must be engaged and interested, not bored or alienated. Developing courses that model diversity by presenting content in an engaging way, using creative graphics and design, and structuring learning activities so that they encourage multiple perspectives is definitely the foundation.

Situated Learning in Online Courses

"Situating" the learning in an online course can mean the difference between success and failure, and can be the key to enthusiasm, high rates of participation and completion, substantive comments in the interactive elements of the course, and engaged interaction. Situated learning is also critical for deep learning and transformative thinking.

"Situated learning" is a term popularized by Lave and Wenger (1991), and it refers to the kind of cognitive activity and knowledge acquisition that takes place in an apprenticeship-type setting. It emphasizes the following elements: content, real life, and mentoring. It involves developing an awareness of both tacit and explicit knowledge. Situated learning is on the other end of a continuum of learning that would place rote memorization on one end and team projects on the other, and it requires the application of concepts to solve problems, provide explanations, and to develop action steps and strategies. An important element in situated learning is social interaction.

To practice a situated learning instructional strategy in face-to-face instruction may be fairly easy to bring about by means of group or team projects which emphasize the production of an outcome that can be displayed or presented. For example, in a recent course entitled Creative Problem-Solving, the students self-selected and formed teams.

The teams were then charged with the goal of developing a strategic marketing plan for a Japanese department store as if they were, in actuality, a group hired to be a "turn-around" management team, to generate new revenue streams by increasing sales to American customers (while not alienating their loyal Japanese clientele).

To be successful, the students needed to apply techniques for creative problem-solving within a context that needed to be analyzed in terms of cultural, psychological, economic, sociological, and geographical contributing factors.

Ethnography, human relations, marketing, and strategic planning were the various disciplines. However, they quickly situated themselves within the limits of the task at hand. By negotiating the desired outcome, the individual learners situated themselves within the complex task at hand. Some conducted market surveys, others looked at store layouts, advertising strategies, and merchandising decisions. Others looked the plan in terms of organized steps that fell into a sequence. The details, action steps, and outcomes were negotiated in a social, dynamic manner which encouraged individuals to draw upon individual as well as collective experience.

Teams formed, and individual roles emerged as strengths and weaknesses were identified and place within the context of the problem at hand, and the desired learning outcome. The data that was collected and presented to team members was "read" in a new way -- through the lens of the tasks at hand and the achievement of goals.

The results were stunning -- not only in the outcomes (complex, high-quality plans, first-rate presentations, outstanding self-awareness and meta-cognitive gains in terms of applying the approach to other similar intellectual problems) but also in terms of student satisfaction. Process elements were also positive. Students posted substantive and thought-provoking responses on the discussion board, responded in respectful and meaningful ways to each other, did additional research (self-guided and motivated), and processed their information. Process elements were also positive: substantive discussions, annotated bibliographies done by the participants, building an annotated bibliography.

On the surface, it would seem fairly simple to replicate this approach in the entire online environment. The "practical" or "project" approaches can be done through collaboration.

A Failure to Situate

However, in the online environment, learning is often not situated well for three main reasons:

1. Incomplete understanding of the nature of the needs, goals, and expectations of the e-learners in a particular group;
2. Failure to select learning activities that respond to the actual context or setting, or a recycling of old, non-updated content);
3. Poor sequencing of tasks or activities, and thus a failure to provide scaffolding.

A Strategy for Situating Learning in an Online Course

Effective situated e-learning requires the following elements:

1. Needs Assessment. This is vital in order to understand how to motivate e-learners and to select content and activities that connect to experiences.
2. Alignment of content. Make sure that the content is relevant to the tasks, and that it provides scaffolding.
3. Experience-Based Learning. Encourage connections with current, past, or collective experience through"
   a. Reflective writing
   b. Discussion topics that make connections between course content and experience
   c. Discussion topics that encourage sharing of experience
   d. Guided discussion responses that reward appropriate sharing of experience
   e. In-depth looks at specific examples (Barton etal, 2000)
   f. Meta-analysis of the particular in order to get at the general, or universal
4. Readings / Texts
   a. Provide conceptual frameworks
   b. Provide theoretical underpinnings
   c. Discuss how to apply concepts to case studies
5. Virtual Teams. Develop projects or group activities that require that individual members of teams prepare components of a report, then share.
6. Encourage social identity production through the team activities.

       a.   Build a narrative about a problem that encourages role-playing
       b.   Encourage teams to be flexible and let identities or roles emerge
       c.   Role-playing is agreed-upon and mutually understood by team members

7. Build in a sense of relevancy and urgency
       a.   Choose topics that mean something to the team members
       b.   Develop a solution-centered approach
       c.   Allow new topics to be proposed that connect to e-learners' real-life issues and challenges

8. Embed theory and/or conceptual tools (statistics, etc.) in the experiential activities so that they are a part of the problem-solving or thinking process, not something outside and unrelated.

9. Encourage self-awareness of the fact that a specialized language is being developed in the groups as learning activities are centering around experience and experience-based tasks.
       a.   Lists of terms and definitions that connect to the tasks
       b.   Specialized uses and applications of terms
       c.   An awareness of the new way that signs, symbols, activities are being "read" -- through the lenses of the context and goals (rather than the other way around) (Gee 2004).

As e-learners engage in a focused, situated type learning in their courses, new internal practices will emerge, and knowledge transfers will take place, not only in the "nuts and bolts" content areas, but in the way that individuals solve problems, think about themselves in relation to a group or a task, and shift their ideas about themselves and others. It is often a subtle shift of orientation and thinking, and yet the outcomes are vastly different in a course that has incorporated situated e-learning.

CITED WORKS AND USEFUL RESOURCES

Barton , D., Hamilton , M, and Ivanic, R. (2000). *Situated Literacies: Reading and writing in context.* New York : Routledge.

Gee, J. P. (2004). *Situated Language and Learning: A critique of traditional schooling.* New York : Routledge.

Lave, J. (1996). Teaching, as learning, in practice. *Mind, Culture, and Activity* 3: 149-64.

Lave, J. and Wenger, E. (1991). *Situated Learning: Legitimate peripheral participation.* New York : Cambridge University Press.

Virtual Internships for Online Business Classes: A Project

Colleges and universities are engaging in virtual projects with developing countries throughout the world. Such projects give faculty an opportunity to collaborate with their peers, to conduct research, and to strengthen their organizations. Students who enroll in virtual internships or who participate in the project are able to gain experience in employing "appropriate technology" e-solutions in places where information sharing, education, training, and community and health support are desperately needed. Funding for such projects may come from transnational organizations such as the United Nations, or various relief or developmental agencies. The following example could be used for a business or information management class which seeks to help rural microfinance institutions in the "South" or lesser developed nations.

The Elements in a Virtual Business Class Internship / Collaboration Project to Use Web-Based Education in Rural Microfinance Institutions

Web-Based Resources Open to the Public
a Multi-use, multi-function web-logs for collaborations, information sharing, announcements, press releases, public relations
b Website portal pages and/or a site map that shows an inventory of resources, including links to directories, library resources, training materials, white papers, technical assistance. Some are sites that are linked would be password-protected. Others are available for sharing, particularly ones that contain "yellow pages" type directories and calendars of upcoming events.
c Portal for gateway to shared or collaborative information. This would include bulletin boards, announcements, threaded discussion boards, and public weblogs.

Web-Based Resources with Private Access Only
a Proprietary information and information resources
b Log-in and access to central server to the central information hub, which would include high-level applications (accessed remotely from personal computers and network hubs using thin-client software)
c Information management / project guidance through integrated customized "umbrella organization" portal
d Financial services provided via out-sources services -- payments, funds transfers, etc.
e Resource bartering provided via e-store, e-commerce solutions
f Open-source courseware for online training and education // distance collaborations

Web-Based Resources Open to Public in "Lite" Version, Restricted Access to "Full" Versions
a Virtual library of white papers
b Training materials: worksheets, procedure and policy guidelines, legal forms
c Educational materials: lessons, educational materials, workbooks
d Curriculum and online courses

Information and Resource Networking
Philosophy: The primary objective is to utilize a team effort in order to share resources, gain insight, enable programs to work effectively, and to train local and regional personnel. Sustainability is emphasized, as well as the development of productive linkages.

-Step 1- Directory of microfinance institutions
The directory provides online information for individual who often have difficulty locating information. It should be made available in English as well as the language of the country.

-a- Provide address, overview of services
-b- List key contacts
-c- List of loan products, services, support
-d- One-paragraph overview of the economy and communities served
-e- Overview of growth areas / challenges

-Step 2- Set Up Virtual Libraries
Virtual libraries allow the sharing of valuable information. Ideally, the interface for uploading will allow qualified individuals to classify the article and upload it onto the correct directory on the server.

-a- Develop a classification scheme, or numbering / filing protocols
-b- Organize existing white papers, technical manuals, documents, online journals, etc. within the classification scheme developed earlier
-c- Create a portal page with site map
-d- Develop protocols for meta-tags and links
-e- Determine which directories and files are to be password protected
-f- Develop "lite" versions of information to be made available for free
-g- Create forms and templates to be used in training and in the administration of loans. Examples include loan worksheets, loan flowcharts, secrets to successful lending and borrowing, borrower's handbook.

-Step 3- Weblogs
The weblogs are intended for the individuals at the individual microfinance institutions to stay in touch with each other, and to communicate with the virtual interns.

-a- Administrator selected for weblog
-b- Categories of topics selected
-c- Links to other blogs
-d- RSS feeds established
-e- Contributors selected to write weekly updates and provide information releases on new developments

-Step 4- Microfinance Institution Cooperation and Collaboration Task Force
By establishing a task force, concrete projects can be identified and implemented. Ideally, the participants will make a commitment that virtual internship lead to ongoing cooperation.

-a- Select participants from regional centers and mentoring university
-b- Define responsibilities and identify achievable goals
-c- Set deadlines
-d- Develop tactics, with an action plan and concrete steps - assign individuals to complete the tasks

-Step 5- Training and Education
The transfer of skills, knowledge, and philosophy is not possible without a robust training solution. It is not economical without utilizing online resources.

-a- Onsite training with access to distance expert who responds to specific issues, provides customized guidance
-b- Online / distance training
-c- Hybrid solution, with materials and curriculum downloaded from the internet with facilitators onsite
-d- Distance consultants provide feedback via chat and e-mail during the onsite part of the training.

Adding Sims and "Serious Games" to E-Learning Now

The "Serious Games Summit DC" have brought home the fact that simulation, in some form or another, should be a part of all online programs, higher education and corporate training. This article discusses how to incorporate free or commercially available serious games and sims in one's online courses and programs, and the kinds of instructional strategies that are most effective.

The first summit was held October 18-19, 2004, in Washington, DC, and it attracted a standing-room only crowd of game developers, military contractors, and representatives from various industries, including health, communications, education, financial services, transportation, and manufacturing. Although the focus of the summit was on developing "serious" games (games that transcend entertainment and are used in industry or the military), there were indications that a sea change has already occurred, and the question is not whether or not serious games (or sims) are effective, it is how to most effectively deploy them. Cost-effectiveness is always a consideration, and many games are now available on pda and gameboys. Case in point is Guidance Interactive's Glucoboy (R), which will be discussed more at length later in this article.

Although video games and simulations have been around for a long time, the interactivity and the fact that they can be multi-player, with the ability to modify the simulated environment makes them more useful than ever, particularly in training teams, or utilizing team-based training. According to Jim Piggot, CEO of Team-Play Learning Dynamics (TPLD, Ltd.), the ideal "serious game" needs to be multi-player or at least use AI to created a simulated decision environment. Needless to say, this is not very effective if avatars can't be modified or customized, and if cultural beliefs and potential knee-jerk reactions can't be introduced by the players. The game needs to be "smart," with the ability to "learn" (in other words, be trained based on patterns). That said, for team-play to be most effective, there must be surprise elements; which is to say that randomness and unpredictability are vital. Entrepreneurship and safety education were mentioned as amenable to interactive multi-player serious game development, particularly if the goal is to raise awareness of causal relationships, likely outcomes, and potential catastrophes.

One of the most hyped serious game is one intended for children, and is to be played on a Nintendo Game Boy. Actually, to call <u>Glucoboy</u> a game is a misnomer. Actually, it is simply used as a data collection device, which rewards the user for entering data and for achieving target levels by activating games. The intended users are sufferers of juvenile diabetes, whose behaviors need to be influenced in order to keep them maintaining healthy blood sugar levels. Glucoboy encourages children to check their blood sugar levels, to maintain a healthy level, and to be aware of the dangers of allowing their levels to get outside a desired range. It is an ingenious combination of cognitive and behaviorist strategies.

Based on the level of interest and the types of presentations made and arguments presented, one could start to make a case that serious games (and even not so serious ones) can be incorporated into all kind of learning environments, with positive results. With the multiplayer, distributed aspect of things, it could be possible to have a "sim" unit accompanied by a discussion board, where students share their results, insights, and responses to guided questions.

ER: The Video Game (Legacy Games - PC)
This is a narrative-driven video game based on teh television series. With a release date of October 25, 2004, it one of the latest of games based on television series, including reality television. The narratives could provide students with an opportunity to explore medical ethics, discuss appropriate medical procedures, and explore human behavior under stress.

Cold Case Files (Activision, Inc.: Release September 14, 2004)
Criminal justice courses could be beefed up with content and multi-player interactions as individuals follow the narrative to

solve the cold cases. Along they way, they could learn about forensics, legal proceedings, affadavits, evidence-gathering, rules of evidence, abnormal psychology and deviancy, sociology, and creative problem-solving.

Flight Simulator - FS Flight Ventures (Abacus - Release October 5, 2004)
This would provide one with a basic familiarity with instrumentation and the concepts of flying.

Rollercoaster Tycoon 3 (Frontier Developments, Inc.)
Zoo Tycoon (Microsoft)
Tycoon games are great sim games, spawned from the original mainframe computer games utilized in engineering and marketing courses back in the 1970s where teams would manipulate variables to see what the consequences of widget marketing and widget manufacturing decisions would be in a multi-player environment. With Sim City and all the worlds after that, sim games became big, big, big -- especially those that combine fantasy (theme parks are perfect for that) and humor (hence, the zoo). Both of these games would be perfect in entrepreneurship classes, as well as strategic planning, creative problem-solving, and team-building.

The Political Machine
Needless to say, the life expectancy of this game is down to almost nil, but doesn't everyone want to be a virtual Lee Atwater (of Bush / Dukakis fame), or Karl Rove? Political strategy takes a back seat to understanding semiotics, the impact of image, the manipulation of stereotypes and cultural truisms, and media-inflected and constructed reality. This is a great complement to psychology, political science, sociology, public relations, and English (cultural studies / rhetoric & comp) courses.

Law and Order: Justice Is Served (Legacy)
The narrative is this: "A talented tennis player is found dead before the start of the U.S. Open. It is your job to follow the clues, put together the evidence, and convict the killer. You'll be helped by detectives from Law and Order." The easy decision would be to use this video game in conjunction with criminal justice classes to help illustrate forensics, legal procedures, and criminal law. However, it could be a perfect complement to an

English composition course which requires individuals to make a case and support their conclusions or hypotheses with evidence.

Virtual U: http://www.virtual-u.org
This is a free sim game, downloadable from the website. In it, the player is the president of a university or a college and must increase enrollments and maintain profitability.

Small Ball: http://www.smallball.com
The players must manage and train a baseball team. Although this is not necessarily multi-player, it could be made collaborative by assigning teams to decide key decisions. Also, each week could have a new scenario, guided by an instructor. For example, the facilitator could require students to sign certain pitchers, or make certain questionable decisions. Then, the players could choose how to compensate for the bad decisions. Discussion boards could allow individuals a place to share.

Mobility: http://www.mobility-online.de
This is an absolutely outstanding free download for courses that require students to understand the complex world of logistics, and how they relate to economic development. The game asks players to make decisions to solve economic and transport problems within a sim city or environment.

Wall Street Challenge: http://wtc.wallstreet-challenge.com
Virtual Trader: http://www.virtualtrader.co.uk
Although Wall Street challenge focuses on New York, and Virtual Trader is British, both games allow players to explore the intricacies of stock trading, and to understand what various terms mean and how they play themselves out in real or simulated situations. Of course, it's better to learn with sim money than real money, so I'm thinking that this game would be even better than assigning extra points for joining a student stock market association, or something of that nature. One can also start to gain an appreciation of one's tolerance of risk, and trading styles.

Tom Clancy Splinter Cell in an Online Course

In a move I thought would be evocative of business or industrial engineering courses that use multiplayer games to simulate market and product competition environments, I decided to integrate an Xbox video game, *Tom Clancy's Splinter Cell,* into an online International Relations course, "Geopolitical Brinksmanship." It required a shift of instructional strategy, and it became necessary to clearly define various roles. Little did I suspect that the approach have more in common with the way that the military utilizes games such as *Full Spectrum Warrior* to familiarize individuals with conditions they may face in battle. It also is reminiscent of how such games help individuals begin to be able to envision scenarios, the potential players, and possible lines of action.

In developing an instructional strategy to achieve course objectives, it was necessary to determine whether or not students should engage in Role-play or Goal-Based simulations. Briefly speaking, a Role-play simulation allows students to enact situations in a safe and supportive environment. Goal-based simulations involve role play, but the focus is less on the context, the people, and their highly customizable behaviors and responses, and more on successfully bringing about incidents or activities that lead to desired end. The "end" of a role-play simulation can occur when time is up. There do not have to be winners or losers. The winning is in the depth, breadth, and relevancy of the interactivity. In contrast, in Goal-based simulations, there are clear winners and losers. For example, winners are those who liberate hostages, destroy documents, secure buildings, and bring back money.

Role-Play Simulations: For the purposes of the course, role-play simulations are more relevant than goal-based ones. Although rescuing hostages, securing the embassy, and destroying top-secret documentation helps motivate students and propels the story forward, it is not the ultimate outcome. The goal is to become familiar with a wide range of issues, which involve national security, political action, economic development, natural resources management, international relations, and psychology. The role-splay simulation environment encourages risk-taking and innovation, as well as built-in "rewards" for creatively approaching issues in order to encourage other participants to "stretch" in their roles. Role-Play simulation, as Albert Ip has pointed out, does not require icons or a graphical interface. It can be totally text-based, which offers certain advantages when flexibility is required.

Goal-Based Simulations: Goal-based simulation also rewards creativity and innovative thinking, but in a way that is more action-oriented (toward an object or series of objects) rather than toward people.

The objective of the course is to develop help learners develop creative problem-solving strategies; the tactics involved working through a series of scenarios in an entertaining and relevant context. Although *Tom Clancy's Splinter Cell: Pandora Tomorrow* is a shooter game, the fact that it is a multi-player as well as a single-player game reinforces the notion "shooting" is part of the game's "grammar." Shooting is a metaphor for communication; it is a way to involve the non-verbal in an environment (online) that tends to be highly restricted in its communication options. The graphics encourage the players to envision themselves in a certain time and place, and the fantasy-building aspect encourages individuals to not think of themselves as limited by real-world constraints. Although there is a definite down-side to fantasy and the attendant problems of invincibility, when one is trying to encourage unlimited "box-less" thinking, the video game can be absolutely liberating.

In order for this to be useful for learners, an instructional strategy needed to be implemented, which included the following:

1---Background reading on the geopolitical issues, general international relations and political science theory, new tactics and equipment
2---Clear descriptions of problems to be solved
3---Suggested problem-solving approaches, ideally collaborative, and using a worksheet so that people can compare

approaches
4---A discussion board to post ideas and to share approaches
5---Collaborations / team papers; facilitator has to assign roles; each role has a separate task to then bring back to the group.
6---Synthesizing tasks at milestone points. Short papers that reflect upon what has been accomplished, and which report the innovative approaches used in problem-solving are useful.
7---Diagnostic self-assessments. Reflecting upon successes and less that useful strategies is very useful, particularly in scaffolding, and developing approaches to be used to build on previous knowledge.

The Game:
The website describes the scenario in this way:
2006: The U.S. installs a temporary military base on East Timor to train the developing defense force of the "world's youngest democracy." Resistance to the U.S. military presence in Southeast Asia is widespread and passionate, but the threat Indonesian militias pose to East Timorese democracy is deemed sufficient justification. At the same time, the U.S. doesn't mind having an excuse to install active military personnel within easy reach of both North Korea and the largest Muslim population in Asia.

Anti-U.S. resentment comes to a head under the leadership of guerrilla militia leader Suhadi Sadono, acting with the unofficial support of major corrupt factions of the Indonesian government. Suhadi's men attack and occupy the U.S. Embassy in Jakarta, taking dozens of civilian and military personnel hostage.

You are Sam Fisher. You're sent in, not to rescue the hostages, but to destroy top-secret documentation held in the embassy before Suhadi's men access it.

Keeping Focus: Probably the biggest challenge in this course is keeping the groups' focus on problem-solving and not lapsing into simply playing the game for entertainment. Instructional strategies need to be constantly refined in order to meet needs and challenges, and to accommodate individual differences between groups and cohorts. Overall, the integration of gaming into online course development proved to be successful.

Useful Articles

Interview with James Paul Gee: "The Learning Game - Researchers Study Video Gaming Principles that Apply to Education"
http://www.wistechnology.com/article.php?id=243

"High-Score Education"
http://www.wired.com/wired/archive/11.05/view.html?pg=1

"Educators Turn to Games to Help"
http://www.wired.com/news/games/0,2101,59855,00.html

"Why Study Rome When You Can Build It?"
http://www.technologyreview.com/blog/blog.asp?blogID=1376

University of Wisconsin Team Creates Learning Games
http://www.wistechnology.com/article.php?id=958

Video Games Gaining Clout as Military Training Tool (2000)
http://www.nationaldefensemagazine.org/article.cfm?Id=352

Prensky, Marc. Selected URLs and other resources for Game-Based Education, e-Learning and Training Game-Based Education Portal
http://www.marcprensky.com/dgbl/Prensky%20-%20Selected%20URLs(web).htm

Management Issues in the E-Learning Organization

What Keeps E-Learning Organizations Stuck in "Catch-Up" Mode?

Since the publication and almost universal adoption of best practices statements backed by such organizations concerned with maintaining standards and publicizing benchmarks, a number of researchers, academicians, students, and online program administrators have started to identify gaps in the best practices, particularly as they apply to 100% online programs, blended solutions (part online, part face-to-face) and multi-delivery method 100% distance (audio-enhanced, etc.).

In the analysis below, the following categories derive from numerous checklists and best practices created by organizations such as Sloan-C, Western Interstate Commission for Higher Education (WICHE), the American Council on Education (ACE), the American Distance Education Consortium (ADEC), and others to help one determine an institution's readiness to successfully develop and deliver distance education.

While the categories are very useful in identifying strengths, weaknesses, and needs, when considered in conjunction with other best practices and benchmarking, they also give rise to possible gaps. These are not always straightforward or easily remedied gaps, but ones that typically span several categories, making it much more problematic to effect a quick fix or simply intervention.

Committed Institution

Overview. The learning organization must prioritize distance and flexible learning, and in doing so, must demonstrate support that is realistic, appropriate, timely, and expandable for the future.

Possible Gaps.
---Program "force-fit" to institutional mission.
In their eagerness to offer online courses and programs, institutions may force-fit the program to the institution's vision and mission. The vision and mission of a university may be grounded in face-to-face interactions, and the philosophy that

underlies the instructional strategy may require an environment that the faculty and staff understand only in terms of face-to-face instruction, or in traditional bricks and mortar arrangement. This becomes problematic because it creates a **culture gap** within the institution.

Although there may not be open resistance, the institution could find itself confronting underground backlash, and troubled with factions, divisive camps, and a breakdown of the vision itself. In this case, the institution must remember that it is reshaping the vision, and for it to be effective, all stakeholders must have buy-in. In other words, they need to have a role in shaping it, and mapping it to their own lives and agenda.

---Revenue generation perceived as more important than the education experience provided.
Although there are few people who believe this any more, the early days of online education were typified by the academic equivalent of get-rich schemes. Later, it became clear that the initial investment of online courses can be steep, and it requires ongoing maintenance and operating expenses, as well as what can be quite steep costs for instruction and student services. When expectations are not met, there is a tendency to try to retrench and cut costs. What results is a focus on costs rather than quality. Further, it becomes tempting to outsource services and to obtain open-source content that has not be reviewed or adapted to one's own instructional and institutional goals.

Learner-Friendly Environment

Overview.
Students, faculty, and other users find the services provided by the learning organization easy to use, accessible, and thorough. The learning organization provides online services such as registration, records, bursar, and library access. Technology utilized is up-to-date and appropriate for the user's actual environments and work patterns.

Possible Gaps.
---Ambiguous needs assessments. A successful online or hybrid program requires clear and realistic alignment with learner needs. In order to accomplish this objective and to attune

courses and delivery with learner needs in the present (and not the past), it is important to utilize multiple methods of collecting data to gain understanding of the needs of the students. Current needs are important, as are what are projected to be important needs in the future. Focus groups, online surveys, random surveys, and interviews are effective methods and should be done on a regular basis.

---**Always a half-a-beat behind the technology curve.** It is false economy to have outdated technology, or to think that investing in online infrastructure is a one-time expenditure. Some of the most common ways that institutions find themselves behind the technology curve are:

-Insufficient bandwidth, and no plan to do "edge computing" to "load-share" surges in volume.

-Old, unworkable home pages and portals, with outdated java applets, javascript, etc.

-Old websites using out-of-date plugins (old versions of flash or shockwave, etc.)

-Failure to update software, holding on to old versions of learning management systems.

-Failure to hire adequate numbers of appropriately trained staff, support staff, and faculty.

---Mass-produced courses. Developing courses quickly, efficiently, and at the lowest possible cost becomes the most important issue, rather than providing the flexibility required in order to produce a course that is not just a bundle of information, but a true learning experience.

---Unwittingly producing training, not higher education. Problem-solving, analysis, synthesis, and critical thinking skills are cornerstones of higher education, and the various stated outcomes that one finds in college-level courses display these skills. However, it is easy for colleges to fall into the trap of producing an e-learning experience that requires little or no actual synthesis of information, and which does not make connections from one discipline to another. Further, courses often fail to provide scaffolding for more future courses.

---Flexible delivery modes should stress multiplicity of modes. It is tempting to succumb to an "all or nothing" approach and to offer courses in only one delivery mode. However, learners need flexibility in order to accommodate their lifestyles and the reality of work, travel, access, and schedules. Thus, institutions must be able and willing to offer not only face-to-face instruction, online, and hybrid, but also variations that include CD-ROM and PDA (or pocket PC) for mobile computing. Content should not be confined to the visual, but should also incorporate downloadable audio, such as mp3 files (podcasts).

---Lack of a plan, or coordinated instructional strategy. Because many institutions find themselves playing "catch up," they are often scrambling to deliver what students say they want (or at least what they wanted six months before). In a "catch-up" situation, institutions lose their ability to plan effectively, and find themselves correcting mistakes made because of moving too fast, and without a coherent, well-mapped out and coordinated plan.

---Jumping on the latest delivery mode bandwagon, even when not appropriate. Institutions waste time, money, delivery efficacy, and faculty competency when they jump onto a trend without doing a thorough needs assessment, SWOT analysis (strengths, weaknesses, opportunities, threats), or a clear analysis of their capabilities and capacity. As a result, institutions have found themselves trying to produce and deliver streaming media classroom lectures, synchronous chat and whiteboard lectures, interactive video game-based simulations, even when neither they nor their students have the bandwidth, computing power, or access to really be able to do it. This does not even begin to touch the problems of instruction in that sort of environment, with such high-power needs, and such a steep learning curve for instructors.

---At-risk students left behind. The online environment can be a sink-or-swim world where only the hardiest and most adept learners stay afloat. It is important to accommodate all learning styles, and to understand the real environment and conditions of learning of at-risk students. This is not simply a matter of making things ADA compliant. It means creating instructional strategies and activities that build community and camaraderie, do not require "extreme" technical skills, and which give individuals multiple ways to do the same task.

---Failure to conduct objective periodic program reviews. The successful launch of an online program is usually accompanies by a huge sigh of relief, coupled with a state of near catatonia (or post-traumatic shock syndrome) over the next several months, even years, as faculty, staff, and information system support seek to recover from the shock of close encounter with "disruptive technology." However, this fails to take into consideration that the nature of disruptive technology is to change the way that people think about tasks, and how they approach it, now that the technology has changed. In order to be successful, it is imperative that one continue to look at one's goals, vision, mission, and desired outcomes and to determine how those have been affected by the technology and the delivery approach.

Faculty Support, Capacity, Training, Mentoring, Compensation

Overview.
Faculty members teach and develop courses in areas where they have demonstrated expertise, experience, and/or leadership. When asked to instruct courses, faculty are provided support, training, and guidance in a proactive manner. Compensation is fair, and intellectual property issues are settled in a manner that is mutually agreeable.

Possible Gaps.
---Failure to provide timely and appropriate mentoring and training. Not only do institutions fail to provide mentoring and training, they also fail to require instructors to undergo the training. In failing to do so, they do the instructors a disservice, particularly in a world that is increasingly dominated by a class of distance professors who have taken the time and effort to equip themselves with the latest equipment and skills to be effective online / multi-modality instructors.

---Failure to review faculty credentials and evidence of growth.

In part, this is a legacy of a tenure system that allows professors, once tenured, to become complacent, or to "retire on the job." It is also a case of expediency. It is not easy to find professors who are early adopters, or who keep themselves up-to-date with technology. They can be good facilitators, but are they staying current in their subject matter? Or, are they continuing to inform themselves of best practices and effective methods to achieve desired learning outcomes? Further, if an institution requires evidence of growth, they have an obligation to support it materially, philosophically, and psychologically.

---When flexibility becomes rigidity. This is a paradox that it, unfortunately, not uncommon. Institutions that start out being flexible by offering students the opportunity to take online courses, may, in fact, become rigid as they invest in learning management systems, templated courses, and a "one way only" instructional design / subject matter expert model for developing courses, and then require the professor to teach in one certain way, to accommodate the technology rather than learner needs.

Psychological Climate in Online Learning Organizations

"We had started calling our online course production department "The Revolving Door," because things had gotten so bad. We couldn't keep student support staff if our lives depended on it. They used to stay with us until they graduated. Now, some would bolt as soon as the semester was up. In the meantime, they would call in and leave long, detailed voice messages about the various maladies that afflicted them. It was horrible. I just hope that this semester will be better." Kelsen, the manager of support staff for the department's online programs was describing the situation in the office. The tension in her voice was notable, and she twisted a piece of paper in her hands.

"It didn't make sense. Enrollments were at an all-time high, we were getting all sorts of positive publicity, and we had been approved for an increased budget. We had money for professional development, new equipment, even travel for professional development. Yet, all I heard was bickering."

Why is morale so bad when business is so good? Many institutions experiencing a boom in their online course enrollments are confronting this issue. Because of the rapid growth and rate of change that characterize most online learning programs, morale within the support staff, faculty, and administrative personnel tasked with developing, delivering, and maintaining the courses and the infrastructure may be very low. Vroom's expectancy theory helps explain it, as does the concept of "psychological climate." This article explores the theory and applies it to the online learning program.

For many years, V.H. Vroom's 1964 classic, *Work and Motivation*, has been pointed to as a model for how the expectations that individuals have of their workplace, their coworkers, and their employer, can deeply influence motivation. In the second edition of *Work and Motivation,* Vroom writes that "the choices made by person among alternative courses of action are lawfully related to psychological events occurring contemporaneously within the behavior" (Vroom 1982: 14-15). In other words, there are psychological "laws" that govern the way a person feels and acts.

Kelsen's experience supported what Vroom found. "It starts with absenteeism, but then we see bad communication, turf wars, divisive and destructive talk, and finally, they simply leave. Then, we spend the next first half of the semester training the replacements. Once they've gotten trained and have spent a month or so being fairly productive, they're out the door. I'm going crazy." She looked down at her backpack. "I even bought a pack of cigarettes and contemplated taking up smoking."

Vroom goes on to articulate his "expectancy theory": "The force motivating a person to exert effort or to perform an act in a job situation depends on the interaction between what the individual wants from a job (valence) and the degree to which he/she believes that the company will reward effort exerted (expectancy) on that job with the things he/she wants. Individuals believe that if they behave in a certain way (instrumentality), they will receive certain job features (Vroom 1982)." This definitely helps explain why it is so important to not arouse expectations unnecessarily, and that if managed well, expectations can be huge motivators, and can connect to one's behavior and/or performance.

Recent studies have expanded Vroom's expectancy theory, and have pointed out that expectations have a great deal to do with how the "psychological climate" is formed in the workplace. The psychological climate, which can be positive or negative, is made up of various aspects which contain expectations. Lawler and Suttle (1973) developed various categories of expectations, and many researchers, such as Darden, Hampton and Howell (1989) and Sims, Szilagyi, and McKerney (1976), further connected them to leadership qualities. According to Litwin and Stringer (1966), leadership style is critical in managing expectations and one of the most important determinants of psychological climate.

In 1988, researchers Good and Sisler conducted a study of individuals in retailing to determine the components of psychological climate. Here are the resulting categories:

Role clarity

Role harmony

Job autonomy

Job variety and challenge

Job importance

Role assignment

When Kelsen heard the description of psychological climate, she gave a wry smile. "Yes, that's precisely it. We have a very toxic psychological climate. I'm not proud of it, but that's what it is. I'd like to know what to do."

She also related to later studies. For example, Woodard, Casill, and Herr (1994) completed a study which required employees to rank the components of psychological climate and to assign relative importance to each one. The results are strikingly applicable to the management of an online program team which includes support staff, administrative personnel, faculty, and administration. Here they are, with comments that make connections between the original results and apply them to the online learning organization:

#1---Role Assignment: Team members are given sufficient time, training, and resources are provided to perform an assigned task so that it is clear what outcome is expected of them.

#2---Role Harmony: Employee receives information about what is expected of him or her in the execution of the job, and it is compatible with job expectations; and later, when detailing the behaviors involved in the performance of the job, expected behaviors are consistent with the employee's understanding of

the job. The job expectations, requirements, and desired outcomes are clearly spelled out and updated regularly. Models of successful behaviors and outcomes are provided.

#3---Role Clarity: Expected role behaviors have been clearly defined to the employee, and everyone involved has the same expectation. When cross-training occurs and teams blur turf and responsibility areas, the opportunity for all team members to discuss roles and responsibilities is provided and leadership focuses on continuity and stability.

#4---Organizational Identification: In reviewing his or her role in the organization, employee believes his/her organization performs an important function, and in doing so, offers unique opportunities for growth and reward, resulting in the fact that the employee takes pride in the organization. Risk-taking is encouraged, and if an idea does not work, team members are encouraged to explore how their expectations were different than the outcome, and how lessons learned can help salvage or repurpose the results.

#5---Leader Goal Emphasis and Work Facilitation: The supervisor encourages and stimulates individuals to become personally involved in meeting group goals by stressing high performance standards, creating an atmosphere that rewards high performance, and then participating in the work himself or herself, therefore setting an example. The leaders does not co-opt or deliberately outperform the individuals.

#6---Job Challenge and Variety: Individuals are encouraged to use their skills and abilities on the job, and their initiative is rewarded as they engage in a wide range of behaviors on the job in order to meet objectives. Individuals are encouraged to share their unique approaches, and to heighten a sense of affiliation and accomplishment through sharing their experiences.

#7---Leader Trust and Support: The supervisor takes the time to become aware of the needs of the subordinates, does not co-opt or distort what the employee I s saying to him or her by misinterpreting, ignoring, or punishing open communication.

The supervisor is both aware of and responsive to the needs of his/her subordinates.

#8---*Workgroup Cooperation, Friendliness, and Warmth:* The working atmosphere is open, and relationships are characterized by cooperation, sincere friendliness, and warmth.

#9---*Management Concern and Awareness:* The organization attempts to assess and respond to the employees' needs and problems. This is done frequently, and response times are quick.

In conclusion, the idea of psychological climate can be a breakthrough strategy for online learning organizations suffering from low morale, high turnover, loss of coordination, communication and teamwork problems, despite experiencing huge growth and financial success.

Kelsen said that her next step was to try to develop a strategy for cleaning up a bad psychological climate. "I'm afraid it's not going to be easy. I'm going to do some research and give it a shot, though," she said.

References

Adams, J.S. (1965). "Inequality in social exchange" In L. Berkowitz (ed.) *Advances in experimental social psychology* (Vol 2). New York: Academic Press.

Anderson, C. H. (1984) "Job design: employee satisfaction and performance in retail stores," *Journal of small business management,* 22:9-16.two studies supported the self-determination model, in that workers' perceptions of their supervisors' autonomy support and the workers' individual differences in autonomous orientation independently predicted the degree to which the workers were able to satisfy their needs for competence, autonomy, and relatedness on the job, which in turn predicted the workers' performance ratings as well as their well-being, indexced by vitality and the reverse of anxiety and somatization" (Deci et al 2001).

"Self-determination theory posits that there are innate psychological needs for competence, autonomy and relatedness, which implies that satisfaction of these three needs would promote motivation and well-being in all cultures" (Deci et al 2001)

Atkinson, J. W. (1964) *An Introduction to motivation.* Princeton, NJ: Van Nostrand.

Bandura, A. (1982). "Self-efficacy mechanism in human agency." *American Psychologist.* 37: 122-147.

Bandura, A. (1986) *Social Foundations of thought and action: A social-cognitive view.* Englewood Cliffs, NJ: Prentice-Hall.

Deci, E.L., Ryan, R.M., Gagne, M., Leone, D.R., Usunov, J., Kornazheva, B.P. (2001) "Need satisfaction, motivation, and well-being in the work organizations of a former eastern-bloc country: A cross-cultural study of self-determination" *Personality and Social Psychology Bulletin.* 27 (8): 930-942.

Good, L. K, Sisler, G. F., and Gentry, J. W. (1988) "Antecedents of turnover intentions among retail management personnel", *Journal of retailing.* 64(3): 295-314.

Herzberg, F. (1966). *Work and the nature of man.* Cleveland, OH World Publishing Company.

James, L. A. and James, L.R. (1989) "integrating work environment perceptions: explorations into the measurement of meaning," *Journal of applied psychology,* 74(5): 739-51.

James, L.R., Hartman, A., Stebbins, M.W., and Jones, A.P. (1977) "Relationship between psychological climate and a VIE model for work motivation" *Personnel psychology.* 30 229-54.

Jones, A.P., and James, L.R. (1979) "Psychological climate: dimensions and relationships of individual and aggregated work environment perceptions," *Organizational behavior and human performance.* 23: 201-50.

Hofstede, G. (1980) "Motivation, leadership, and organization: Do American theories apply abroad?" *Organizational dynamics.* 9: 42-63.

Kelly, J.P., Gable, M. and Hise, R.T. (1981) "Conflict, clarity, tension, and satisfaction in chain store manager roles," *Journal of retailing.* 57(1): 27-42.

Lawler, E.E., III (1973). *Motivation in work organizations,* Monterey, CA: Brooks/Cole.

Lawler, E. E., III, and Suttle, J.L. (1973) "Expectancy theory and job behavior," *Organizational behavior and human performance,* 9: 482-503.

Litwin, G.H., and Stringer, R.A., Jr. (1966) "The influence of organizational climate on human motivation," *Foundation for research on human behavior.* Ann Arbor, MI.

Locke, E.A., and Latham, G.P. (1984). *Goal-setting: A motivational technique that works.* Englewood Cliffs, NJ: Prentice-Hall.

Locke, E.A., and Latham, G.P. (1990) "Work motivation and satisfaction: Light at the end of the tunnel," *Psychological Science.* 1(4): 240-246.

Lucas, G.H., Jr. (1985) "The relationships between job attitudes, personal characteristics, and job outcomes: a study of retail store managers," *Journal of retailing,* 61(1): 35-62.

Pearson, C.A.L., Hui, L.T.Y. (2001) "A Cross-cultural test of Vroom's expectancy motivation framework: An Australian and a Malaysian company in the beauty care industry" *International Journal of Organizational Theory and Behavior.* 4(3&4): 307-327.

Ryan, T. A. (1970) *Intentional behavior.* New York: Ronald Press.

Sims, H.P. Jr., Szilagyi, A.D., and McKerney, D.R. (1976) "Antecedents of work related expectancies," *Academy of Management Journal,* 19: 547-59.

Strang, H.R., Lawrence, E.C., and Fowler, P.C. (1978). "Effects of assigned goal level and knowledge of results on arithmetic computation: A laboratory study." *Journal of applied psychology.* 63. 446-450.

Vroom, V. H. (1964) *Work and Motivation.* New York: Wiley.

Vroom, V. H. (1982) *Work and Motivation,* 2nd edition. Malabar, FL: Robert E. Krieger.

Woodard, G., Cassill, N, and Herr, D. (1994) "The relationship between psychological climate and work motivation in a retail environment" New York: Routledge, 297-314.

The Bare Necessities: Pivotal Conditions for Blended and Distance Learning

Let's imagine that there exist just three "pivotal conditions," and let's consider how those conditions might fit into the goal of determining how to make effective learning environments (face-to-face, online, blended, and my new favorite -- "pod-blended"). Face-to-face instruction refers to traditional classroom delivery and online refers to 100% Internet or web-based delivery. Blended learning indicates a hybrid mix – part face-to-face, and part web-based, while "pod-blended" indicates a multi-delivery mode mix, of portable data devices (iPods, pdas), multimedia, online, and face-to-face. There is no prescribed ratio or distribution of delivery modes.

1--- Flexible environment that allows the facilitator to respond to learner needs.
Face-to-face: The syllabus creates a structure, with an emphasis on learning outcomes, rather than a rigid obsession with marching through content. This allows the facilitator to conduct ongoing needs assessments in an informal manner, and adjust accordingly, to assure relevance of discussions and content. Group work expedites the process of discovering the needs of the learners, as well as the best configurations for collaborative work.

Online: Because learners develop what could be thought of as "ambiguity anxiety" when they are working online, it is very important to have a clearly defined structure. However, it is important that the structure is not too rigid. The online environment is flexible when the facilitator is able to clarify, add discussion questions, encourage collaborative activities, and post illuminating and relevant articles. It is also flexible when students are able to post and upload items in order to share in a meaningful way, tapping into the energy of weblogs, collaborative space (comments, etc.), and wikis.

Useful article: Carol Twigg's "Innovations in Online Learning: Moving Beyond No Significant Difference," published in the

Pew Symposia in Learning and Technology, held December 8-9, 2000, in Phoenix, AZ, and published in 2001 by the Center for Academic Transformation at Rennselaer Polytechnic (Troy, NY), contains a number of interesting and relevant insights with respect to flexibility and a learner-centered approach. In the section entitled "Improving the Quality of Student Learning," it is pointed out that "a fundamental premise of the symposium is that greater quality means greater individualization of the learning experiences for students" (9).

While this is still undoubtedly true in 2005, the burden is not so much in the facilitator-student interaction, but in the constellation of learning activities that can be modified to achieve desired (and clearly identified) learning outcomes.

2--- Content developed with a view to providing theoretical underpinnings.
Face-to-face: Although classroom activities result in discussions that focus on specific readings, issues, or problems, they are most productive when all are mindful of the theoretical groundings and the principles that support the "learning by doing" or the "situated learning." Such an approach allows students to create generalizations and universal applications to specific experiences. It also creates the common thread that gives learners an ability to communicate with each other and learn from similar experiences. Improved self-efficacy and self-concept are natural outgrowths of this constructivist approach.

Online: Translating a dynamic, "learn-by-doing" experience-based-learning environment into an online learning space is not easy. Often one finds that there are "disconnects" between the collaborative activities or the experience-based discussions and tasks, and the instruments used to assess learner mastery of the content and skills. How does one bridge the gap? How does a multiple choice test fail to assess the broad spectrum of general and specific knowledge gained in a "situated learning" based environment?

One strategy is to tap into the rich semiotic environment of the e-learning space and to utilize icons, graphics, and visual representations. A theoretical framework is often most effective when it is laid out graphically, in a way that makes the connections between activities and underlying theory extremely transparent.

Although the facilitator will guide students to an ability to work with the organizing principles that underpin the readings, discussions, and learning activities, the student should have a conceptual framework clearly in mind. This is often most effective in the online / distributed environment when diagrams, lists, and tables provide a graphical representation of the information, and a well-organized bibliography anchors it.

Even though we may be conditioned to think of online learning as something that occurs when seated at a laptop, with the learning looking into the monitor, it is important to recognize that the paradigm is shifting away from that. More content is being accessed through pdas that have web access, but which can also store data through pdf files (Palm, Treo, Blackberry). Individuals are now downloading audio content and playing them on portable audio players, most frequently iPods.

With that in mind, it is important to make connections between content, concepts, and illustrative points or vignettes. For example, it may be important to present information to learners in the form of concepts / news bites, followed by a story / vignette, and then a question-and-answer session. Radio programming that comes to mind that would illustrate this would be National Public Radio's All Things Considered (http://www.npr.org/), with vignettes reminiscent of This American Life (http://www.thislife.org/). Finally, engaging question and answer sessions can be presented in the manner of Calling All Pets (http://www.wpr.org/pets/).

It is very exciting to think of the ways that distance learning is evolving, and the directions that mean that the costs of access could fall dramatically, or at least result in more efficient use of resources, with extreme portability.

Useful article: Nada Dabbagh's "Distance Learning: Emerging Pedagogical Issues and Learning Designs" Quarterly Review of Distance Education 51 (1), 2004, pp 37-49, contains an invaluable table which maps instructional strategies to pedagogical models and learning technologies (47).

3--- Communication and interaction-friendly environment

Face-to-face: Although traditional face-to-face learning environments have long been characterized by a pedantic "sage on the stage" who "holds forth" in a lecture mode, for the last 20 years, the reality has been quite different. Even where there are large lecture presentations, this constitutes only a small part of the classroom activity. Much is done in small labs or in discussion groups, containing 8 – 15 individuals and a facilitator. The perceived authority of the facilitator is mediated in this environment, and there is more of a focus on the discovery and presentation of outside information.

Online: Making sure that communications are purposeful and learning outcome-focused is the responsibility of the facilitator. In addition to guiding students so that they respond to certain questions pertaining to the content being discussed, facilitators help individuals find strategies to overcome the limitations of the sometimes rigid and/or overly deterministic semiotic realm of the discussion board.

Effective communication builds student self-efficacy, and helps students learn by doing, and master skills on their own (situated learning).

As students interact, the effective facilitator should be able to identify and intervene to repair holes in scaffolding and do it for learners in an individual manner.

Useful article: M. J. Hannifin, etal, discuss the way that students learn to develop strategies for organizing, interpreting, and internalizing knowledge when they engage in interactions via technology, and via interactive multimedia. What is perhaps most interesting about this article is the way it anticipates the emerging trend to expand "hybrid" to include not just face-to-face and site-based multimedia (a television or a computer), but also portable devices. Their article is entitled "Student-centered learning and interactive multimedia: Status, issues, and implication" in Contemporary Education 68(2), 94-99.

Annual Check-Up for Your Learning Organization

At least once a year, it is important for a learning organization to evaluate itself by means of well-designed surveys. If you can develop diagnostic instruments that tie not only to best practices in one area, but incorporate vision, values, and project management philosophy with tactics and strategy, you will have a better idea of whether or not your organization is accomplishing its goals and heading in the right direction.

Without a procedure for systematically analyzing or assessing one's online programs, courses, and administrative support, an institution is likely to encounter fairly intractable problems associated with growth and/or technological change.

Your surveys should be designed to have the following characteristics: a) provides almost instantaneous results by being easy to use; b) does not require an initial cost or investment; c) can be applied to users across the organization; d) improves coordination between an institution's units; e) assures online program / course tie-in to the organization's mission and vision; f) pinpoints areas that need immediate attention; g) facilitates a gap analysis by prioritizing needs and allowing one to suggest low-cost remedies; h) identifies programmatic strengths in order to build on them.

Think about focusing your first survey on learning effectiveness. This may present a problem if you have not clearly stated your desired outcomes. On the other hand, the lack of well-defined and specified learning outcomes could be a positive finding, and could lead to a clear idea of how to remediate the program. Keep in mind that you are striving for an integrative approach that requires close coordination between all stakeholders and participants, whether they are located in (or between) academic and administrative functions.

As you develop a survey instrument, or questionnaire, to administer in all units of your learning organization, be mindful of how it will be administered. Make sure that the approach is easy for everyone to understand. Also, keep in mind that you will have data to process. If you can develop an online survey that automatically tallies results, that will save you many valuable labor hours.

If the questionnaire is easy to use and administer, it is likely to be adopted across the institution. It is important that decision-makers and key implementation personnel in each unit participate. All stakeholders in the organization should be given the opportunity to critically analyze learning effectiveness from their point of view. Divergent opinions and visions will allow the organization to gain insight into the actual state of affairs.

Developing and Implementing an Affordable In-House Survey:

The questionnaire you develop should cost very little to implement and should not require an extensive investment of time or training to administer.

By being easy to implement at a very low cost, the organization begin to evaluate its program and approach in an integrative, across-the-institution manner. Ordinarily, this would be complicated and could involve expensive or conflict-engendering approaches. The diagnostic tool avoids that potential pitfall.

Improved Coordination:

The development of the questionnaire is the first step, and all stakeholders in the organization should be involved.

By involving stakeholders on every level of the organization, from implementation to administration, effective communication is established, particularly as individuals discuss the questions and review the results. Task forces can be established, and effective planning can be built on a foundation of concepts that are commonly understood by all.

Mission and Vision Tie-In:

Develop questions that revolve around your organization's mission and vision. Be specific. How does each area of your organization connect to the mission and vision? How are their activities helping achieve the central mission?

The questions in the diagnostic survey instrument are designed to raise one's awareness of how the online program and courses connect to the institution's vision and overall mission statement.

The importance of this cannot be overstated: whether or not an institution achieves its objectives depends precisely on how it implements the mission and vision within each aspect of its online program. Learning effectiveness can be measured by means of outcomes assessments and development appropriate metrics. However, if the mission and vision are not somehow applied to the learning outcomes, then the overall effectiveness cannot be determined in any meaningful manner. While discussing results of the survey on learning effectiveness, the units are able to communicate with each other how they achieve the tie-ins to the institution's vision and mission.

Pinpointing Areas that Need Attention:

Perhaps one of the most important results from the survey instrument is the fact that it allows the institution to pinpoint problem areas with a fairly high degree of precision.

One problem, however, is that you might be tempted to focus too much on the details and miss the big picture.

However, a close look at areas that need attention, with appropriate levels of detail also gives individuals in different units the opportunity to discuss remedies and to explore the reasons for potential issues. This is a triage approach, which is very valuable because it allows units to be aware of where the problems are and to determine the severity of the problem, and at the same time, encourages a dialogue about the nature, origin and impact of the problems.

Getting from Point A to B:

After you collect your data and analyze it, you should embark on an analysis of needs and shortfalls. A successful implementation of your diagnostic survey instrument, followed by discussion and analysis of the questions, the results, and the proposed remedies facilitates a gap analysis.

Briefly put, a gap analysis is a detailed look at the status of one's program (as determined by the diagnostic tool) as compared with the ideal status. Where does the organization want to be? Where is it at this point? The difference is the gap. Where are the small gaps? How is the gap closed? By prioritizing needs and allowing one to suggest low-cost remedies, the institutional units can close the gaps. The initial diagnostic survey instrument helps set the institutional units on the right path to real results.

Identified Strengths as a Foundation:

Develop questions that help you determine the strengths of your institution and the online program.

Then, make a list and rank the strengths. The make a list of the weaknesses. Which ones could be fatal to the organization or the program?

One benefit of this approach is its identification of strengths as well as weaknesses. The areas of the program that are most operationally effective are revealed. Where the institution is most clearly achieving its strategic goals becomes very clear. In developing action steps, particularly in conjunction with a gap analysis, the organization can follow the model established by the successful units or areas that are achieving maximum learning effectiveness. Building on success and strengths will allow the organization to present a unified front, and to coordinate development across academics, administrative support, and information technology. It also allows the organization to develop effective training and support for learners, facilitators, and subject matter experts.

Leadership and the Future of the E-Learning Organization

Creative Partnering: Build Alliances, Student and Faculty Base, Diversified Cash Flow

1---Education Providers: Divide courses and instruction, focus on the strengths

2---Professional Organizations and Associations: Tailored curriculum, hybrid with ACE-approved materials

3---ACE-approved Training and Professional Development:

4---Affiliate Programs for Diversifying Cash Flow for Complementary Products and Services:

5---Affiliate Program for Promoting Programs, Services, Products, and Generating Traffic:

6---Product Development for Future Markets and Opportunities:

7---Diversified Content Providers (Across delivery modes):

8---Technology for Diversified Delivery Modes:

9---Career-Planning and Placement:

10---Government Agencies, Think Tanks, Institutes, Dignitaries, Public and Private Sector Luminaries

Authentic Leadership and the E-Learning Organization: A View for the Future

Because of the nature of the e-learning organization, marked as it is by constant and perpetual metamorphosis, perhaps the most effective leadership strategy is to employ a combination of charismatic, transformational, transactional, distributive, and authentic leadership. Charismatic leadership will mobilize the organization and the leader will communicate a vision that has the potential to come alive in the hearts and minds of the followers. Transformational leadership emphasizes personal as well as organizational change and growth, while transactional lays out the methods and steps to get from point A to point B. Distributive leadership gives rise to a democratic approach to decision-making and an effective assignment of tasks. However, none of these will work – individually or together – without the "glue" of authentic leadership.

Authentic leadership can be characterized as a leadership approach that seeks to find solutions to problems and to achieve objectives by emphasizing the capacity to empathize and understand the needs of individuals within the organization.

As the leader demonstrates a deep connection to the followers, she or he engages in an ongoing analytical process which aligns team member talents and abilities with organizational needs. The leader then works with team members to develop a plan that is both goal-oriented and flexible. Such a task requires the leader to possess a complex set of skills, with effective, active listening forming the foundation. It also requires what has been characterized as emotional intelligence (Goleman, xxxx).

Later, the leader must demonstrate credibility through showing competence and the ability to set and achieve goals.

To become an authentic leader requires other qualities as well. The leader must demonstrate that he or she

    a)   Possesses the capacity to feel empathy;

b) Has the ability to self-regulate, thus can control emotions;
c) Is willing to dedicate time, effort, and resources to learning the needs of followers;
d) Maintains an approach that is underlain by a widely understood moral foundation;
e) Can break large goals into small, achievable goals, and is willing to work individually with units to have success;
f) Acknowledges the contributions of individuals, and rewards in a timely and appropriate manner.

It has been pointed out that the organizational climate since the 1990s has been such that employee trust has been eroded as company after company demonstrated itself willing to freeze salaries, cut benefits, lay off divisions, and spend pension funds while giving executives and board members huge bonuses, salary increases and stock options.

In a negative environment where leaders are perceived as selfish, greedy, or indifferent, employee trust in the leader is low to non-existent. In order to re-establish trust, there must be "relational transparency." L. Hughes observes that

"Continual activation of an authentic moral leader's values and ethical standards as part of his or her working concept will promote relational transparency" (Hughes, in Gardner, 2005, p. 391).

Hughes continues to by developing a four-pronged approach to relational transparency. It requires a) setting goals; b) developing a vision or identity; c) setting shared values; d) engaging emotions (Hughes, 2005).

Emotions are essentially those involved in an empathic approach to human relations. Not only does is require active listening, it also stresses tolerance, flexibility, and a willingness to engage humor in response to frustration.

Even if an organizational head is truly empathic, and possesses the values of an authentic leader, employees are likely to view the leader with skepticism, if not outright cynicism. Without a results-centered approach and effective goal-setting so that members of the organization can see that the leader is both sincere and willing to assume personal risk to better the lives of everyone, the leader is likely to be considered manipulative, insincere, and perhaps even dangerously deceptive. Thus, the decision to pursue the authentic leadership approach is not without its perils.

However, once he or she has obtained the support of team members, the authentic leader will help guide the establishment of an environment of authenticity. The authentic environment is characterized by an emphasis on strengths rather than weaknesses, and by the presence of positive reinforcement. Although it can be difficult to win over the hearts and minds of employees, the rewards are worth the effort. One can argue that it is perhaps the only approach that will work in a time of rapid change, employee fear and disenchantment, and an unstable business environment.

Reference

Hughes, L. (2005). Developing transparent relationships through humor in the authentic leader-follower relationship. In: W. L. Gardner, B. J. Avolio, and R. O. Walumbwa (Eds). Authentic Leadership Theory and Practice: Origins, Efforts, and Development. Oxford, UK: Elsevier Science.

Biographical Note.

Susan Smith Nash has been involved in the design, development and administration of online courses and programs since the early 1990s. Her current research interests include the use of learning objects, new, popular technologies in distributed education, and leadership in e-learning organizations. Her articles and columns have appeared in journals, and her podcasts and articles on e-learning can be found online in educational weblogs. She received her Ph.D. from the University of Oklahoma in 1996, and in addition to e-learning, Nash has also been involved in international economic development training, and humanities and culture, which has included the promotion of Slovenian literature. Her latest books include *Lonelyhearts Pawn Shop*, published by Light & Dust Books, and *Otozna Boginja,* published by Sodobnost (Ljubljana).

www.ingramcontent.com/pod-product-compliance
Lightning Source LLC
Chambersburg PA
CBHW021553210326
41599CB00010B/419